MANIFESTING AN ABUNDANT LIFE

Through Divine Alignment

MANIFESTING AN ABUNDANT LIFE

Through Divine Alignment

Ushering in The Divine Plan of Your Life and Creating the Life of Your Dreams Though Accessing Divine Alignment and Using Sacred Techniques, Processes and Tools.

By
Rev. Christopher Macklin, Ph.D.

Manifesting an Abundant Life, Through Divine Alignment
Copyright © 2019 Christopher Macklin

All rights reserved. No part of this book may be reproduced in any manner whatsoever, or stored in any information storage system, without the prior written consent of the publisher or the author, except in the case of brief quotations with proper reference, embodied in critical articles and reviews.

ISBN: 978-1-941608-03-6

Printed in the United States of America

Disclaimer: This publication is sold with the understanding that the author is not engaged in rendering psychological, medical, or other professional services. If expert assistance or counseling is needed, the services of a competent professional should be sought.

*To my dearest Amanda,
I am ever grateful for your abundant
spirit and loving heart.*

TABLE OF CONTENTS

Preface……………………………………….......................i
Introduction……………………………………….............vii

Part One/ The Sacred Cosmic Matrix
Chapter 1. Divine Humanity…………………….....................1
Chapter 2. Soul/Higher Self……………………………….7
Chapter 3. The Physical Matrix……………………………...15
Chapter 4. Divine DNA / Light / Water and Sound…………...23
Chapter 5. The Human Biofield……………………………33
Chapter 6. Divine Cosmos-The Sourcefield………………….45
Chapter 7. Unity Consciousness……………………..................51
Chapter 8. The Subconscious Mind/Ego……………..................59
Chapter 9. The Starseeds…………………………….....................67

Part Two / Divine Alignment
Chapter 10. The Divine Plan / Divine Alignment……………..73
Chapter 11. Discovering and Using Your Gifts……….................85
Chapter 12. The Art of Consciously Manifesting / Giving
and Receiving…………………………………....................99
Chapter 13. Beliefs and Self-Created Stories………………...109
Chapter 14. Negative Influences…………………….................121
Chapter 15. Fear, Anxiety, Anger, Depression and Stress……..139

Chapter 16. Change Yourself / Change Your World..............147

Chapter 17. Embracing Your Imagination / Creating A List.....155

Chapter 18. Money……………………………………...............163

Chapter 19. Intention……………………………………….....171

Chapter 20. Intuition and Inspired Action…………….............177

Chapter 21. Focus-The Key……………………………….....185

Chapter 22. Determination / Commitment………….....……..193

Chapter 23. The Company We Choose / No Holding Back........199

Chapter 24. Expectancy / Divine Timing……………………..209

Chapter 25. Faith / Trust / Purpose……………………..........215

Chapter 26. Gratitude and Joy……………………………......225

Chapter 27. Self-Love / Self-Esteem……………………….....231

Chapter 28. Compassion / Kindness……………………….....239

Chapter 29. Surrender and Forgiveness………………….........247

Chapter 30. To Align or Not to Align / That is the Question.....255

Chapter 31. Stepping into Loving Authority / Commanding Your Life into Alignment…………………………………......261

Chapter 32. Time / Timelines / Soul Families……………......265

Chapter 33. Manifesting Vibrant Health / Perfect Relationships / Abundance and Success………………….......277

Chapter 34. You Deserve the Best………………………........283

Chapter 35. Alignment of the Heart……………………….....285

Chapter 36. Creating A Daily Routine……………………....297

Chapter 37. Manifesting At A Glance……………………....301

Part Three / Sacred Prayers, Processes and Tools

Chapter 38. The Sacred Processes and Tools……………...............313

Chapter 39. Intro to the Sacred Prayers / Maps of Intent………315

Chapter 40. The Sacred Prayers / Maps of Intent……………........317

Chapter 41. Meditation……………………………………….......339

Chapter 42. Wisdom Beyond Forgiveness……………………......343

Chapter 43. The Chakras / Chakra Meditation……………..…….355

Chapter 44. Akashic Record Clearing and Meditation…………365

Chapter 45. Activating Affirmations……………………….....……369

Chapter 46. Body Work / Energy Healing Sessions……………373

Chapter 47. Vibrant, Harmonized Living Spaces…………....……377

Chapter 48. Angelic Teams and Assistance………….....…………383

Chapter 49. Sacred Geometry……………………………….............387

Chapter 50. The Great Laws……………………………….....…..403

Chapter 51. The Magi Manifesting Technique…………………409

PREFACE

I remember the day.

I was sitting in a square in Manchester, England…homeless, bankrupt, living out of the back of my car. The two bags at my feet contained all I owned. It was one of the lowest points in my life.

I had previously been a successful IT executive, ushered around in Bentleys, controlling vast financial accounts. One by one, over a period of a few years, situations in my life completely and absolutely fell apart. Twenty-one years of marriage ended in divorce. I had been in charge of whole departments of people. I lost all of this through a series of unexpected events. There I was sitting in a public square, with nothing to show for it and nowhere to go.

It was in this place, one of the most pivotal in my entire life, that I surrendered it all to God.

This is what I knew I had to do.

I had tried my best to keep things together and still they all continued to crumble in my hands and blow away like dust.

I had been born with an extraordinary capacity to heal. Over the years I had developed my potential through using my gifts to help people heal their physical bodies and their lives. It was here, during this devastating and cathartic moment that I received the deepest knowing that using my gifts to make the world better was what God wanted me to do. This was the Divine Plan for my life.

I began to understand that my previous life had fallen apart because I was out of alignment with what I had come here to do. All of this was initially difficult to grapple with but once I solidly understood I was able to move forward.

I made a pact with God in that sacred moment, sitting in that square.

I said to God with total trust and conviction that I would share my healing gifts with the world to the best of my capacity, but I would surrender the way the resources and money came in to God...ALL TO GOD.

After finishing this prayer, I released it all.

From that moment on everything in my world changed. My life took many twists and turns. It took me to unexpected places, where I met people and did things that I would have never imagined. It took me on pilgrimages, through sacred initiations and adventures and finally led me out of the UK. It eventually brought me to America where I would settle down, get married and run a successful healing ministry. Today I do hundreds of healings a week, helping people all over the world heal every aspect of their lives.

These changes resulted because I stepped into divine alignment and allowed God's vision for my life to unfold. My part in this has been to continuously put forth the effort to maintain my connection with the Divine and to use the gifts I was endowed with to uplift the planet. In this way, my life has unfolded as an expression of God's vision. I can honestly say that I am happier now than I have ever been. I love my life and I wake up every day with tremendous enthusiasm for living.

What I know is that the most important aspects of creating the life we desire revolves around staying in the highest frequency we can maintain, following our intuitive leads, honoring divine synchronicities, staying surrendered and using our gifts. This is the formula for divine alignment.

We are the children of God. We are Divine Beings.

God didn't create us to suffer or struggle. It is the divine intention that our lives be continuously joyful experiences filled with true love, vibrant health, financial abundance and successful, satisfying careers. If we are experiencing anything less than this, we have the power to turn it all around and create the life that God has envisioned for us. We can do this wherever we are in our lives, no matter what we are experiencing, young, old, infirm, impoverished. It doesn't matter, we can harness the divine power within and any situation can be completely turned around.

I and many others are living proof of this.

When we step into divine alignment everything changes for the better. Our relationship with the Divine grows and our trust expands. The goodness that God intended for us flows into our lives and out into the world.

Divine alignment is the solution to every problem we currently face. If everyone on Earth was in divine alignment, we would experience a radical shift on the planet. Peace, abundance, vibrant health and loving relationships would be present everywhere because this is what God intended for us all.

It has been said that God gives us the dreams and desires within our heart and the capacity to manifest them. This is true. Using divine alignment, we access the divine plan of our lives. Our creative potential and power and our capacity to manifest good for ourselves and others is activated through this sacred alignment.

Manifesting the positive dreams within us and using our gifts to create goodness in the world is considered by some to be the most important responsibilities of every individual.

In the pages that follow you will find the teachings and techniques that have been a part of my work. Much of what I teach and use has been given to me directly from the Divine and is a part of the Melchizedek teachings from the Ultimate Dimension. It may be completely new in some ways and perhaps familiar in other ways. In the same respect, the uplifting, honest, spiritual teachings of the world all bear similar qualities because authentic, divine teachings all bear a similar imprinted energy.

The energy and wisdom within the Melchizedek techniques is very pure and powerful. It has the unique quality to create change very quickly. Great progress and transformation can be made with proper application. I have witnessed this not only in my life but also in the lives of my clients around the world.

In the pages that follow, you will find a comprehensive study of the art of manifesting. These techniques have been the foundation of my own personal transformation.

It is my sincerest hope that this information assists in transforming a searching, aching world into Heaven on Earth. This is what God wants for us and this is the ultimate goal of divine alignment and the Melchizedek techniques.

God Bless us all,

Chris Macklin
2019

INTRODUCTION

God created humanity to be the Ultimate Being. At one point, we stood in our full glory and knew the truth of our divine birthright. Originally, we were intended to have the power, frequency and impact of the Divine in action. It may be hard to imagine what we were or how we existed at the time of our creation, but the divine seed and intention still lives within us.

Most of the ancient stories, about who and what we are, don't speak of humanity as a divine and exalted race. This tells us how far we had wandered away from our truth by the time these stories were created. The power that created the universe lives within us, and when we are in alignment with it we too can create on vast scales. We have allowed ourselves to be led away from our truth, but it doesn't change who or what we are.

We are created in the image of the Divine. God chose to instill in humanity a vast array of gifts and attributes. One of them is the capacity to manifest our dreams and wishes into the physical world. Most people are unaware of the fact that we are "hardwired" to do this. They are unaware that there is even a process and formula for consciously manifesting, or that each life has a holy purpose.

God designed the 3rd dimensional world to be a classroom, and in any class there is a body of information to be mastered. We have been created with the expressed purpose of evolving our consciousness and expanding our divinity out into the cosmos. While the presence and increase of negativity, to the degree that we see today, was not originally intended; we can rebalance and correct all of this, in ourselves and in our world.

We are creators. In our education here on planet Earth, we are being taught how to master divine alignment, and expand into our understanding of ourselves as divine beings. In any classroom you have various types of people; some who really want to excel and learn the curriculum, some who are not as motivated and some who may not even know why there are there. Many people have no recollection of the fact: this is a classroom and that there is a deeper purpose behind everything. They can't make sense of the world around them or how they fit in. This one missing piece of information causes vast numbers of people to wander aimlessly throughout their lives...never really being able to connect the dots. This is not how God intended things to be. God wants to manifest in a co-creative process with every individual. God wants us to experience all of the beauty, joy and expansion available to us through the divine plan. In order to do this, we must master the process of divine alignment; which is ultimately aligning ourselves with God's will, so that we can manifest the divine intention for our lives.

Many times, people hear about the powerful techniques and laws inherent in the manifesting process; because they have certain beliefs, they have difficulty accepting them. The laws that govern manifesting are just as concrete as the other natural laws, like gravity. Working all of the time whether we are aware of them or not. They don't have an "off" switch. So, what we see around us is the result of the unconscious and conscious creative process of billions of souls, going back untold generations into antiquity.

Inversely, and unfortunately, people have been led to think that they cannot have their heart's desire, achieving their dreams might be impossible and disappointment, pain and violence is normal. In all due respect, people have been conditioned to think this way. Because they think this way, they create this way. The world is filled with billions of people. The majority of them are not consciously manifesting their dreams. But they are, without knowing it, manifesting…all the time.

They don't have knowledge of their own power, nor a true understanding of cause and effect. They can't see the breadth of all of the things they've put into action. They don't consciously understand that they are creating the world around them.

It is time for us to awaken, and relearn the truths inherent within our divine souls.

This book is a comprehensive guide to manifesting the divine plan through maintaining divine alignment. It is separated into three parts. Part one outlines the nature of the sacred, holy, matrix that we live in. It describes how and why we are hardwired to succeed. Part two, outlines the different aspects of accessing and maintaining divine alignment. Part three, contains the sacred prayers, tools and processes that help us evolve and maintain divine alignment.

The book is set up to be read one chapter at a time, daily. There are exercises included to help you integrate and process the main idea, as you go through your day. Move forward at your own pace, but remember that it's ok to spend time practicing and absorbing each idea. If you choose to go through the book with a friend, you may want to really discuss how all of the individual principles are working in your lives, thoroughly, before moving on to the next chapter. Touching base, discussing the ideas and what you are noticing will allow the ideas and energy to expand in your life.

I suggest that you get a dedicated journal to use in this process. If at all possible, get a paper journal as opposed to using computer entries. However, you choose to proceed is fine, but paper is preferred. It will carry the energy of your intentions and your transformation.

Stepping up in your life and reclaiming your birthright will create powerful changes in the world. You will bless yourself and all of creation. When one person awakens to their divine truth, a piece of the cosmos awakens, and it becomes easier for all of humanity to advance.

The truth is that manifesting your dreams is easier than you know. It may be better to look at manifesting an abundant life as a lifestyle change, as opposed to, the acquisition of a few new techniques; to increase your magnetism, and capacity to manifest items or experiences in your life.

We were born to manifest the glory that is within our divine nature. This is true of every living, human, soul on this planet.

It's time to awaken to the truth of our divinity, to become empowered and determined in reclaiming our divine birthright. It is time to live as the divine beings that we are.

Let us choose to lead the most joyous lives possible and offer unconditional love, compassion and kindness to all. Let us embrace the divine power of our immortal souls, and usher in Heaven on Earth.

Abundance is your divine birthright. Happiness is your divine birthright. Wonderful nourishing relationships, wholesome, loving partnerships, vibrant health and fulfilling, satisfying, careers are all your divine birthright.

May we have the motivation, strength, courage and willpower to educate ourselves and find out the truth about who and what we are. May we embrace the life and the gifts that God has given us.

May we have the determination and self-love to heal our lives and restore Heaven on Earth.

PART I

THE
SACRED COSMIC MATRIX

CHAPTER 1
HUMANITY, A DIVINE AND HOLY RACE

Humanity is a divine race, created by God to be the Ultimate Being. We are a powerful and magnificent race with supremely exquisite, unparalleled and unique: emotional, genetic, mental, spiritual and physical qualities that can align with God in co-creation in any moment. A pivotal part of this is the fact, we were gifted with the capacity to express and create using the power of love. Love permeates all of God's creation in its most minute and essential aspects. All of creation can feel and express love, but humanity has been endowed with the capacity to create through using love in the physical in a very specific way. This is one of the things that makes us so unique and special.

Our physical bodies are constantly pulsing out blasts of bio-photonic light and sound that are in every moment co-creating our current reality. We are a spectrum of color, light and frequency. Variations of the rainbow flow from different parts of our being. Energy vortices, commonly known as chakras, located all over the body and within our energetic field: spin, pulse and communicate with one another. They circulate energy and information directly from our souls, throughout the body; and out into the world in a symphony of creativity that is constantly taking place in, around and through us.

Unbeknownst to most people, the energy that flows out from us is capable of manifesting a spectrum of experiences; depending on what we are feeling, thinking and intending.

Most of humanity has experienced a marked drop in consciousness, and cannot comprehend the nature of who and what we are. We have come so far from our truth, and blind to our own power and divinity. One of the most important things we can ever do, is restore ourselves and begin to consciously create our lives. This will allow us to directly experience our own divinity, and capacity to manifest greatness.

We are vast multi-dimensional beings that wield an enormous amount of power. We exist across numerous dimensions; within the same time frame, and within multiple time frames. We have the aspect of ourselves that we know ourselves to be...right here and right now. We also have our inner child. We have our Divine Inner Source Self...the God within...and we have other past and future selves, in addition to many other multidimensional selves.

One of the most important things we can ever do, is to know and believe the truth of who and what we are. This is especially true, when it comes to consciously manifesting; and creating our lives because when we know, believe and experience the truth of our personal divinity. The quality of our life changes exponentially.

Knowing and believing the truth about ourselves, causes us to think and act in different ways; than if we didn't know the truth. We stand stronger. We can do more, and create from a place of pure power and integrity. We understand, that committing our lives to experiencing our relationship with God, allows us to live our truth. God lives in us and through us.

When we set out to consciously manifest and create the world around us, with this understanding, we become the Divine in action. We become grounded to mother Earth, and exalted in the cosmos. It's just as important to stay centered within your divine core, as it is, to honor and appreciate the body; through eating healthy food, enjoying your career and living in a safe, loving home, etc. In this way we learn to love and respect every aspect of ourselves, especially our physical body. We begin to know that everything about our being and body is holy. Laughing and smiling is holy. Washing up is holy. Cooking is holy. Hugging is holy. Eating is holy. Creating art is holy because we are holy.

Approach whatever you are doing as a holy task and the energy will shift, raising your frequency. Inner to outer. As above, so below.

Create balance through embracing your divinity, without any arrogance, without any pretense. All of humanity is holy.

Cultivate a present, centered knowing of this. Experience your life shifts, change and open as you become grounded in the knowing that you are a divine being; and that your life has a sacred and holy purpose.

****

<u>I AM A POWERFUL DIVINE BEING, CAPABLE OF CREATING MY REALITY ACCORDING TO MY HIGHEST JOYS, TRUTHS AND PASSIONS.</u>

****

Exercise #1

PRESENT MOMENT AWARENESS

One of the most potent ways to experience your own divinity; and the divine energy flowing through you, and around you, is to continuously experience the present moment.

Hold the intention, on a daily basis, to experience more of your divine self through staying in the present moment. If possible, set aside 5 to 10 minutes daily on this initially.

You may want to create a practice around it. Just allow your thoughts to exist without trying to block them, and without resisting them. Work to stay in the NOW as author/teacher, Eckhart Tolle, would say. Keep your attention in the present…moment to moment; as opposed to, allowing yourself to get caught up in thoughts about the future or the past. As you cultivate the practice of being in the present, you will experience more of your divine self-expanding. It's a delicious and wonderful experience. You will feel a heightened sense of awareness, peace and spaciousness. Enjoy this feeling. It is the truth of who and what you are.

As you begin to experience more, and more, of your own divine presence; your life will begin to shift. Things will begin to work out, with greater ease and grace, as the Divine expands through you. Breathe it in and stay present through every moment. Enjoy the experiences and transformation.

If you feel led, take out your journal and write about your experiences.

****
You were created to be the Ultimate Being. God rejoices in your awakening.

CHAPTER 2
SOUL / HIGHER SELF

The soul and the higher self, are at the core of our physical embodiment. Our relationship with them, helps us maintain divine alignment and manifest the divine plan of our lives. Through our alignment, with our soul and higher self we are able to bring in the power and vision of God. We have access to our divine essence and birthright in the highest, most organic, natural manner.

The soul and higher self are two different and separate parts of our being that embody within the physical. They carry the wisdom of God and the knowledge of how to manifest Heaven on Earth.

Initially, the soul was housed inside of the higher self, and the energy of the higher self was deeply connected into and through the physical. This connection illuminated the mind, body, emotions and consciousness of the individual with high levels of pure divine energy. When people started making choices which caused them to move out of divine alignment. For example, holding negative thoughts and feelings, and engaging in violence: a form of experiential / perceptual disconnect occurred between the body and the soul / higher self. The higher self and soul, while still connected to the body, do not dwell amidst all of the negativity that some people create. When we choose to consciously engage our soul and higher self again; we begin the conscious effort of restoring our sacred inner matrix, and re-establishing more divine alignment in our lives. We pull all parts of ourselves back into harmony.

We interact with our soul and higher self through intention, imagination and intuition. We engage our soul and higher self through the power of unconditional love, forgiveness, peace and gratitude. We are in the highest alignment with these divine aspects of self; when we make the effort to stay in the highest frequency, and follow our intuition.

Many people around the world today are out of alignment with their soul/higher self. They have no idea of how their whole being is supposed to function in an integrated way. They don't do the things that would promote a healthy relationship with their soul/higher self. At the same time, information has been lost or hidden; in reference to our relationship with our higher self/soul. Because of this, most people don't understand how these aspects of ourselves help us in creating lasting happiness, joy, balance and alignment.

When a person experiences different kinds of trauma or for whatever reason falls in to a practiced negative state, as mentioned earlier, the larger aspect of the soul may energetically distance itself from the body. This helps the soul to maintain a higher frequency and autonomy while staying in alignment with the higher self. The consciousness of the person may become more negative as a result of their choices and behaviors. In the same respect, some souls have been altered through conscious manipulation, repeatedly lowering the frequency, or unhealthy, low vibrational experiences. Sometimes the soul can become fragmented and pieces may be lost, taken or left in places or with other people. If this is the case, it may take some work to restore the soul. And at the same time this situation is more common than most people know.

When a person passes on, they come before God and review their life. If forgiveness wasn't given during their life, they experience what they have created and then they are forgiven and their karma is reset. They review whether or not the soul experiences or lessons were met and then they go on to choose which experiences/lessons they will have in their upcoming life. In this context, we can see how important it is to interact with our souls so that we can be aligned with its intention for this life. This is an incredible asset to have. You will create far more satisfying and successful experiences when you understand what your soul has come here to do.

As we move into greater levels of alignment we have to make the effort to take care of and honor all aspects of ourselves especially our soul and higher self. They are a direct interface to God. They bring in more personal power and increase our capacity to do good. They expand our awareness of the bigger picture, helping us to understand the divine intention and how to manifest it.

With their help we begin to understand two extremely important aspects of living: spiritual maturity and self-responsibility. Spiritual maturity means that we must take responsibility for our creations and our lives. We can do this in many different ways but ultimately we do this through expanding our consciousness, staying in the highest states of awareness and taking the actions needed to insure that we are living honestly, honorably and authentically. Staying connected to our soul/higher self helps us walk upon the earth as the fully capable, responsible, unconditionally loving, compassionate, divine beings we were created to be.

When we imagine and visualize positive ideas and outcomes our soul takes this information and creates different ways for us to manifest these things. Our divine selves are committed to creating positive experiences and beneficial outcomes for all. This is why whenever we seek to create in a loving balanced way we have automatic support from Source. Inversely, when we create from greed, arrogance or negativity, we usually find life filled with more difficulties and blocks. We step out of alignment, out of the flow and into adversity. We don't receive the same kind of support from the universe when we turn away from it.

The soul and higher self-functions from the perspective of unconditional love, surrender and unity consciousness. When we respect, honor and align with these principles, we are able to step into and maintain divine alignment.

When we consciously harness the divine power that already lives within us, our frequency rises, our personal power increases, and we begin to access the divine plan of our lives consistently with far greater ease and grace.

Choose to intentionally stay connected to and influenced by your soul and higher self. Intentionally bring your soul and higher self in to all of your activities, projects, career choices, relationships, financial decisions, business endeavors, recreational activities, etc.

Allow your soul and higher self to bless not only your life but all of creation.

In doing this we become the conscious stewards of our lives and of the Earth once more. We experience God more completely. Our energy and frequency stay in a heightened state. What we experience and attract into our world changes to reflect this consistently higher vibration.

Communicate and sing with your soul. Receive the wisdom and love from your higher self. You will experience more positive movement within your life and in your creative process. Working with your soul/higher self will propel you forward in your manifesting process.

We were not meant to live a life that isn't directly influenced by our soul/higher self. It is our responsibility to do this work and to heal, restore and rebalance ourselves if and when we experience an inner disconnect. Our soul and higher self are always available to help us step into the ocean of unconditional love and the divine plan of our lives that is our divine birthright.

****

EMBRACING MY SOUL AND HIGHER SELF ALLOWS ME TO COMPLETELY TRANSFORM MY LIFE.

****

Exercise #2

Take some time soon after you wake up to sit quietly. Take some deep breaths and ask God to bring you into alignment with your soul and higher self in a way that you understand so that you can communicate with them.

In a way, it would be similar to taking time to understand the feelings of your heart.

When God brings your higher self and soul into your awareness, spend time becoming familiar with them and getting to know them so that they can integrate further into your life and help you.

Listen to their guidance and receive their nurturing love, care and assistance. Notice the transformations that happen in your life from spending time with them. Allow them to help you access and maintain divine alignment.

Daily communing with them will hasten your evolution and speed up the integration of the divine plan into your everyday experience. Your life will be charged with Source energy and love. You will live as the divine being you were created to be.

****
The light of your soul and higher self-illumines the world.

CHAPTER 3
THE HOLY PHYSICAL BODY

The human body is a divine vessel that has a consciousness and intelligence of its own. As we center into our divinity and alignment we do not move up and away from the body, we ground down into and through it, connecting to the Earth. It's through embracing the body that we manifest and enjoy our lives. Some people have felt like they were trapped in a body but the truth is that the body is divine and has been designed to help us evolve and experience greater freedom and power.

In the ancient Vedic healing traditions of India there are accounts of yogis (yogi, meaning…. one who practices yoga and yoga, meaning…union with God) who have been able to elevate the frequency of the body, causing it to vibrate at higher and higher rates. As the consciousness of the yogi expands, the capacity of the physical body to function in various ways increases. Through the trappings of our modern lifestyle, we have actually lowered the frequency and vibration of the body, decreasing its capacity to function as it was intended. However, looking at the Vedic traditions we gain an understanding of how versatile, sensitive and capable the body is. In some cases, as a person's consciousness and frequency increases people have been known to be able to do all kinds of things with the body such as levitate, manifest more than one body to do spiritual work and teleport. Paramahansa Yogananda's "Autobiography of A Yogi" is an excellent read for anyone interested in learning more about some of the body's incredible gifts and abilities.

The body is the completion of our emotional matrix. The subconscious permeates, informs and co-creates the physical body. The biofield or auric field surrounding the body creates the different attributes and qualities the body takes starting at conception. Information from the higher self and soul can be felt throughout the body, and in specific, in the solar plexus, via our nervous system where a ganglion of nerves converges there to receive and transmit energetic messages. We have "intuitive feelings and knowing" that we experience in the body, especially in that region. When people say they have "a gut feeling" this is what they are referring to. Another example of the body's intelligence is when someone gets the chills or gets the tingles. Usually this is a message of affirmation for people. Something will happen and in response ….as a positive signal from the body... the person will experience the chills.

The body is covered with energy vortices of varying size and strength called chakras. There are both major and minor chakra systems. The major chakras run along the spine in the energy body, as well as above and below the actual body. The minor ones can be found in the hands, the groin, within the torso, along the clavicle and around the elbows and ears, etc. These energy centers are constantly receiving and transmitting energy to and from the soul and the Divine into the physical body. When they are working properly, they are charging the body with Source energy. This has a huge impact on how the body functions and is able to navigate in the world.

Chakras govern and affect every aspect of life. They oversee how we exist in the body…from our capacity to stay grounded on the planet to our capacity to give and receive love. They directly relate to how well we are able to support and sustain ourselves and how well we can flourish. It's of vital importance to keep the chakras clear and running smoothly in order to optimize the physical body and life experiences.

The body is constantly in the process of renewing and regenerating itself from stress and toxins. At the same time, we are constantly breaking the body down through harmful behaviors, poor eating habits, toxins, addictions, sedentary lifestyles, exposure to microwaves, ELFs, EMFs and negative emotions, thoughts and relationships, etc.

Taking care of your body, loving it, respecting it, and keeping it physically healthy, including getting plenty of rest and eliminating stress is important and helps the body to actualize its full potential.

The body is an extension of the natural world. It has an amazing capacity to receive and transmit information and energy. People are constantly being given information via the body. They don't typically understand that messages are coming through the body nor do they know what they mean. The more we become aware of the fact that the body is continuously communicating with us, the more we can use the information and tune into our inner wisdom. The body's messages are vitally important. The better we are able to understand and honor them, the better life gets.

Holding the intention to be aware of the information that is coming to us through our body will fine tune this skill. The body can signal us as to how to proceed in different situations, who to spend time with and even what foods are right for us at different times, etc. If you don't already honor your body's messages, begin to sense purposeful feelings and ideas that come through the body. This is very real information to help us take care of ourselves. Cultivating a heightened sensitivity and responding to these messages encourages them to continue in a definitive way.

For example, you may have an idea to do something and with that idea you suddenly have a strange pain or a stomach ache. Noticing these body cues will allow you to realize the body itself is giving you guidance. Usually, pain would be interpreted as a "No, not a good idea". If you eat something and soon after you start to cough, it may be that your body is telling you that the food in question isn't suitable for you at the time. In addition, some people practice kinesthetic testing or muscle testing, which is a way to utilize the information coming from the body to assist you in your life. The more you practice noticing and receiving these cues, the more these cues become increasingly apparent.

Our body is our divine vessel. It was created to hold the essence of God. It is the part of ourselves that allows us to manifest in the physical and on the Earth. Love your body. Cherish it. Cultivate positive thoughts about it. Appreciate where you are in it and allow it to grace you with the light and love of its divine composition. Most of us have wandered so far away from being able to live in joy in our bodies. The return to divine alignment is through the body. The more you assist the body to stay in alignment the more your capacity to help yourself increases. Take good care of it. Honor and appreciate it for all it does.

It was created to help us fulfill the divine plan of our lives.

Many of the things we are seeking to manifest on Earth would hold no purpose if we didn't have a body. Let us shower it with love, joy and gratitude.

****

<u>I LOVE MY BODY. IT IS THROUGH MY BODY THAT I ENJOY THE DIVINE PLAN OF MY LIFE.</u>

****

<u>Exercise #3</u>

Pull out your journal and make some notes. Take time to review how well you are caring for your body. Are you loving and accepting of it? Are you honoring and respecting it? Is there anything you could do for your body that would allow it to feel more love?

Is there any place where you could care for your body better?

Please take time to show the body that you love and appreciate it on a daily basis. As you increasingly love your body you will feel better and you will notice the quality of life will increase. With this your vibration will rise and your capacity to manifest goodness will accelerate.

Take time every day for at least 5 minutes to think of something that makes you truly happy. It could be people you know and love. It could be the sunset. It could be a young child, an animal companion or even an activity that makes you happy. Helping your body feel the energy of happiness and joy daily allows the body to shift, change and restore itself.

Hold the highest ideas about it and allow it to be the best and most it can be in any moment.

****

THE FURTHER I MOVE INTO MY BODY THE FURTHER I MOVE INTO MY DIVINITY.

CHAPTER 4
DIVINE DNA-LIGHT, WATER AND SOUND

We are beings who are emitting bio-photonic light and sound via our DNA at all times. In addition, the body is nearly 70% water. This water, light and sound within us is attenuated to the vibrations and frequencies we hold in our consciousness. They are deeply affected by our thoughts, feelings and intentions.

Dr. Masaru Emoto, a Japanese researcher, photographer and author, in his groundbreaking studies on frequency and water, was able to demonstrate how our thoughts and feelings affect the water in our bodies and in our environment. He taped a series of different words to jars of water and froze the water. He understood that by doing this the energy of the word would alter the structure of the water because every word has its own unique frequency and vibration. Water absorbs energy information. It is like a hard drive and it holds whatever information it is exposed to.

Dr. Emoto used the same kind of water in each jar. Each jar of water had a different word taped to it. Once the water was frozen, each jar emerged full of water crystals that were unique to the word that was taped to it. Each word created its own unique crystal. The results were stunning. He took pictures of all of the different crystal formations and published his findings. The implications that emerged were obvious. Our choice of thoughts, words, feelings, intentions and deeds are deeply affecting the energy, structure and health of our bodies which again, are roughly 70% water.

The jars which had positive words attached to them, i.e., love, joy, harmony, gratitude, compassion, etc., all had absolutely gorgeous, high frequency, crystal formations. Other statements like, "You disgust me" or "you fool" created distorted, garbled, gnarled formations in the frozen water, painful to look at but incredibly important in what they revealed. If we are thinking negative things about ourselves or others, or if we are in relationships with others and they are saying or thinking these things about us…all of this is having a tremendous effect on our physical structure and make-up.

The water in our bodies is listening to what we are thinking, feeling and saying.

It's important that we think and feel positive thoughts towards ourselves and others. In this way, we keep the water in our body healthy and positively charged and we assist others to do the same.

If something should come up where we experience pain or trauma, it's important to process and honor what you are feeling in the moment. Work through it so that you can release it.

When we take responsibility for caring for ourselves and clear the sad, negative or stuck emotions from our system, our bodies become stronger and we are able to stay healthier.

Dr. Emoto's photographs provide concrete examples. They allow us to see what we are doing to ourselves by giving us visual examples of the frequencies we are generating in the water within our bodies.

Dr. Emoto's photographs can be found online at
http://www.masaru-emoto.net/english/water-crystal.html.

The state of the water in our body also deeply affects our DNA. This in turn dramatically affects how and what we are manifesting.

Our DNA is more complex and more important than we have been led to believe. It is the creator and projector of our physical reality, blasting out bolts of biophotonic light and sound in a never ending series of patterns. It is literally building the structures of physical creation. It not only helps create the physical body but it also helps us to create our physical reality and our lives.

The nature of how our life out pictures and the quality of our life stems from our consciousness and how we hold our energy. Our frequencies, thoughts, intentions, vibrations and emotions move out into the physical through the DNA. The DNA then creates light and sound frequencies which project into our body and out into the environment around us and manifest according to the ideas and frequencies we hold in our consciousness.

The DNA is nourished and fed by the water in our bodies. It needs to be well hydrated in order to work properly. One of the problems in today's modern society is that most people are extremely dehydrated, in general. This is because of all of the toxins in the food, air and water. The increasing levels of stress, anxiety and depression also affect the DNA.

When the DNA is stressed and dehydrated our whole process for manifesting in the physical is altered. The DNA tightens and constricts and doesn't function optimally. When we nourish the DNA through healthy sources of water, happy emotions and positive thoughts, the DNA relaxes and expands.

It's extremely important to avoid GMO foods because these mutate, damage and genetically modify our DNA. We have developed food and water re-vibration prayers which help to clear and re-calibrate the food and water we consume. You can find them at the rear of this book and also on the Christopher Macklin Ministries prayer app. These prayers were specially designed to remove the negativity and restore the frequency and purity of our food and water.

Our bodies are also created from light. They create, hold and emit light. The biophotons within our bodies give off light that is roughly 10 times lower than what we experience from the regular sunlight during the day.

The nature of the light in our bodies is dependent on the frequency and vibration we routinely hold. Kirlian Photography is able to capture the images of the light we are generating. We can literally see the energy that our bodies and the objects around us are emitting. We see that both living beings and inanimate objects are generating and radiating light and color. It's important to find reputable sites because there's a lot of disinformation on the internet on this subject. If people truly understood that they are made from light and are constantly generating light, they would behave very differently and in general, have a newfound sense of confidence and self-love.

There are healthy forms of light like the sun and full spectrum lighting that help us rejuvenate and make us feel good. There are also unhealthy forms of light which cause us to become weaker and sicker like fluorescent lighting and street lights.

It's important to increase the healthy light we choose to expose ourselves to so that the natural light in us can be fed. It's also important to stay informed about the negative forms of light around us so that we can use our discernment in choosing what we expose ourselves to.

In addition to light, our cells are also creating sound and nourished by sound. In fact, our cells are communicating to each other through sound and the proper functioning of the body is dependent upon this sound. Our bodies are deeply affected by all forms of sound, positive and negative.

We are surrounded by all kinds of sounds on a daily basis, most of which are carrying adverse energies. Much of the modern music is tuned to frequencies that are unhealthy. Many of the messages are negative. In large cities, intrusive, loud sound pollution is everywhere. It creates a destructive impact on our system, bombarding our cells with harmful, low vibrational frequencies.

Because sound creates such a powerful impact on our bodies, we need to be mindful of what we expose ourselves to. The healing sounds found in nature as well as listening to your favorite music will help you to stay in a relaxed and balanced mood while keeping your frequency high.

Just like our bodies, life on this planet is sustained and deeply impacted by light, sound and water. Taking greater responsibility in understanding the building blocks of our physical makeup goes a long way in helping us maintain optimal health so that we can stay in the highest alignment.

Visualize a beautiful divine being made of light, love and sound. The lights and beautiful sounds emanate from its body as it walks along the shores of the ocean. Love flows from its body, uplifting and nourishing all of the world around it. This is the divine human being.

****

<u>I AM CREATED FROM LIGHT, LOVE AND SOUND. I AM A POWERHOUSE OF DIVINE ENERGY.</u>

Exercise #4

Radiating Love

The work of Klaus Joehle has enriched the world in a myriad of ways through his teachings about radiating love. This is a process that can be done at any time. Once you begin to experience the wonderful changes that come from intentionally generating and sending love you will want to do it all of the time. Many people make this a consistent daily practice. They not only radiate love but they also send love to others and to situations in order to help create the highest possible outcomes.

When first learning to do this, find a quiet space where you won't be disturbed. Visualize the energy of unconditional love coming from your heart and filling your body. Expand it out and let it fill your whole energetic field. Continue to experience what it feels like to radiate the energy of love from your heart out into your body and into your energy field. Practice radiating love in stronger and stronger currents. In the same way as when you do breathing exercises, you purposefully circulate the air in your lungs, you purposefully flow the energy of love from your heart allowing it to nourish your body first. Imagine it flowing through every cell. After that, allow it to leave your body. Let it clear and charge your energetic field. As you allow it to expand out from your body you will notice that you will be filled with more and more happiness.

Intentionally work to increase the practice of radiating and sending love.

Practice this first thing in the morning. Practice throughout the day. Make sure to radiate love while you are fixing food. Radiate love when you are walking the dog or washing up. Whenever your mood goes down or something stressful happens, take a few moments, breathe deeply, radiate love and feel your frequency shift.

Staying in the highest frequency possible is the foundation of bringing higher frequency experiences into your life. Many things will change if you practice this exercise consistently.

You may notice that people are suddenly kinder or more attracted to you. You may also notice that situations improve dramatically. Allow yourself to receive. Learn how to monitor the levels of love you are radiating in relation to the activities you are doing. You may want to intentionally radiate more or less love depending on what is going on around you.

Enjoy this extremely powerful tool that can and will immediately change your life.

****

You are an unlimited being of love, light and divine sound. Intentionally bless the world through your presence.

CHAPTER 5
THE HUMAN BIOFIELD

The work of Eileen McKusick, is ground breaking. She has been one of the primary researchers of the human biofield more commonly known as the human aura. Her work in the field of sound and its effect on the human body have totally revolutionized what we know about the biofield, its functions and human healing.

The name biofield was adopted in 1992 by the National Institutes of Health. The coining of this phrase by the medical establishment has allowed people who would never have believed that it existed to understand a critical part of our physiological makeup. One of the things that McKusick has been able to uncover is that the subconscious mind appears to be housed in the biofield or the aura. Incredibly important discovery.

It has been said that if you want to know what you want to create in your life look at what you already have. What we currently have is what we have been able to manifest through the use of our conscious and subconscious mind. It's the best we can do in the moment considering our patterns and beliefs. Subconscious blocks have presented the biggest problems in the process of manifesting and moving forward in life. These often deeply imbedded patterns have been difficult to recognize, heal and dissolve...because they can't clearly be seen. Now with the biofield work we have easier ways to detect, heal and dissolve these blocks.

Through McKusick's research and work she has been able to localize and discover how certain patterns and frequencies reside within the auric field. Her work has found that patterns of trauma consistently flow to the same spot in the energy field. In the same way that the feet are under the legs and the hands are at the end of the arms and the nose is center in the face, so too different frequencies indicative of recurring patterns and experiences consistently reside in the biofield in the same place, person to person. Within the biofield, the area around the right knee is specifically related to obstacles moving forward. On the left side, along the ribs is the side of the mother's energy and the ancestral river where energy from the family lineage is housed, etc.

The subconscious mind holds any resistance and/or blocks to moving forward and experiencing love, worthiness, abundance or success, etc. Now that these incoherencies have been demonstrated to have a physical location in the energy field, this means that they can be addressed and cleared in a much faster way than was previously understood.

McKusick's work has been able to document that the aura is the energetic system that holds the information that the physical body is created from. Thought precedes the physical and our physical being has been created through this energy field that holds all of the stored and accumulated information from our experiences. The biofield surrounds and permeates the physical body.

McKusick has created a map of the human biofield showing where different energetic patterns reside within the field. This is an unprecedented contribution in the studies of the subconscious mind. She has worked diligently to show how the frequencies related to traumatic experiences travel down specific energetic pathways within the field of a person when they are unable to process an experience fully.

What we have known for a long time is that when someone experiences trauma or any sort of pain, stress or violence that they can't process at the time of the event, in order to cope, they store the unprocessed pain and information in the subconscious in order to continue on with life in the moment. Heartbreak, abuse, violence and similar experiences all have to be dealt with, processed and integrated before a person can truly move on and heal. To a large degree the level of consciousness that a person has at the time of the trauma determines how much of the information can be processed, forgiven and transmuted.

A child who has suffered abuse typically is extremely vulnerable when experiencing such a wounding. Usually they don't have a way to process the experience without feeling bad about themselves or making themselves responsible for it. Like fresh clay, the experience makes an impact within the conscious and subconscious mind of the child and creates a molding of the personality. The person deals with the situation as best they can. Stories and beliefs are usually created around what the violence means in order to justify and account for how the experience could have happened. In other words…"This was allowed to happen because I am a bad person and I clearly deserved this." In this way the belief system continues to rest within the biofield as a specific frequency….in a specific place. If other such traumas are experienced, again the portion of the experience that can be processed at that time is processed…and that which can't be processed at that moment is stored in the same area as all of the other traumas of a similar vibration. These vibrations accumulate over time. Should similar kinds of experiences occur…and depending on the kind of life the person leads, they may wind up with a lot of what McKusick terms "incoherencies in the field."

McKusick explains that these incoherencies are created as the trauma impacts the energetic body and pieces of the light body break off into the auric field in reaction to the trauma. The pieces of the light body remain in the auric field until they can be returned and incorporated back into the light body. In addition, when a piece of the light body breaks off, the light body begins to leak light. There is an overall destabilization of the being and the person's frequency is lowered. A new source of light leakage occurs every time there is an unprocessed trauma that causes breakage in the light body. Eventually if the person continues to experience breakages of the light body and incoherencies in the field they can begin to experience increased imbalances which lead to the onset and symptomatology of disease.

Not only has McKusick been able to isolate the places in the biofield where certain experiences are uniformly stored person to person, she has also been able to show how information is stored chronologically. The experiences that have happened to a person most recently will be found closer to the body and those that happened in the past are further away from the body...like tree rings. Those things that happened at birth are farthest away from the body and those things that can be traced to experiences in utero are even further out past the birth experiences.

We begin to see that the biofield is a detailed, vast information database which has accrued all of the experiences that have happened to people not only in this life but in others. Certain information flows along specific pathways which supports the idea that people continue to make certain kinds of choices in their lives and recreate similar vibrational impressions in the field until they reach a point where they have enough awareness, maturity, determination and strength to change the experiences that they are creating and attracting.

McKusick has been able to help people clear the traumas that are stored in the biofield through working with sound therapy. She is able to identify and harness certain incoherent wave clusters and return them to the body, often times into the chakras closest to where the incoherencies reside. The body knows what to do with this random piece of energy that had broken off from it earlier. Once returned to the body, this piece of light energy creates a healing within the body. This missing energetic puzzle piece helps to restore not only the frequency but what McKusick also understands to be the voltage of a person. People have experienced healings in many areas from this process.

Most people today are only looking at raising their frequency and vibration. McKusick encourages people to also think of restoring their voltage. Just as if we have a 9-volt battery that has lost voltage and no longer functions normally, so too we have a certain voltage level that we were designed to function optimally at. When we are not at the appropriate voltage level because we have suffered from so much breakage in the light body we too will not be functioning at our peak levels and can suffer from loss of vitality and functionality. We simply don't have the proper electrical voltage flowing through our system to remain healthy and active.

The biofield research work gives us a tremendous resource in understanding who and what we are. We can see how all of this impacts our capacity to manifest our goals and dreams. In terms of staying in alignment and accessing the divine plan of our lives we have a much needed piece of the puzzle that explains how and why we've been blocked.

The unconscious mind has held all of the big pieces of "how and what" we are able to create. The blocks in the subconscious mind have kept people stuck and continuing to repeat patterns that they have desperately sought to heal and transcend. In the past people have sought out different forms of energy work, traditional therapies and self-help techniques to break through these patterns and blocks. Now with the techniques of the modern biofield specialists and skilled energy healers, we have more direct methods that yield lasting results. We can move forward in our journey of alignment without the patterns of resistance continuing to resurface.

Succinctly McKusick has been able to demonstrate through her research that:
-The field doesn't die and that it accumulates information and carries the information lifetime to lifetime.
-The field is bio-plasmatic and electrical in nature. She states: "We want to surround ourselves with electron givers not electron stealers. We want to keep ourselves in a voltage rich environment. Continue to raise your voltage and carrying capacity for electricity in your system."

Her work reminds us that the whole world is electrical and plasmatic in nature. In order to keep our field healthy, we must keep the energy in it circulating and promote biophotonic health. One of the ways to do this is to stay in the highest frequencies of happiness and joy. If our biofields are clear, then our energy isn't constantly channeling through the clutter and debris from past traumas or stored pain.

Through working with the energy of our biofield directly we can make powerful transformations and heal the parts of ourselves which have needed to be loved, cleared and integrated so that we can move forward.

****

<u>THE ENERGY FIELD AROUND ME CONTAINS THE INFORMATION OF MY SUBCONSCIOUS MIND AND SOUL. I BLESS, APPRECIATE AND FILL IT WITH LOVE AND LIGHT.</u>

****

<u>Exercise #5</u>

The following exercise is a powerful process that comes from the book "Unveiled Mysteries" by Godfre Ray King. I have chosen to include it because it is an amazing asset to use in the clearing and recharging of the biofield.

***

The first step to the control of yourself is the stilling of *all outer activity* of both mind and body. Fifteen to thirty minutes at night before retiring and in the morning before beginning the day's work, using the following exercise will do wonders for anyone who will make the necessary effort.

For the second step: make certain of being undisturbed, and after becoming very still, picture and feel your body enveloped in a Dazzling White Light. The first five minutes while holding this picture recognize and *feel intensely* the connection between the outer self and your Mighty God Within, focusing your attention upon the heart center and visualizing it as a Golden Sun.

The next step is the acknowledgement: 'I now joyously accept the fullness of the Mighty God Presence - the Pure Christ'. Feel the *great brilliancy* of the Light and *intensify* it in every cell of your body for at least ten minutes longer.

Then close the meditation by the command:

> ***I AM a Child of the Light - I love the Light - I serve the Light - I live in the Light - I am protected, illumined, supplied, sustained, by the Light, and I bless the Light.***

Remember always: One becomes *that* upon which he meditates,' and since all things have come forth from the Light, Light is the Supreme Perfection and Control of all things.

Contemplation and *adoration* of the Light compels *illumination* to take place in the mind - health, strength and order to come into the body - and peace, harmony and success to manifest in the affairs of every individual who will really do it and seeks to maintain it."

****
You are surrounded by a field of light which loves and supports you.

CHAPTER 6
DIVINE COSMOS

The entire cosmos and everything in it is made of light. Just like the biofield, it's plasmatic and electromagnetic in nature. It's filled with the consciousness of the Divine. It's alive, awake, aware and present. It's always in motion, always expanding, always responding.

It's exquisitely sensitive and we affect and interact with it through our energy, intention, frequency and consciousness. Energy follows intention and attention and our thoughts, behaviors and emotions are manipulating the field.

This is worth repeating:

Our thoughts, emotions and behaviors are manipulating the source field of our world, the cosmos.

The clearer our biofield, thoughts, feelings and intentions, the more we affect the source field in a positive way. The more joy and love we hold in our hearts, the more satisfying and happy our experiences are. Our lives become easier. This is because the source field and our life mirrors back to us what we send out.

When we lower our vibration, we step out of alignment with the divine plan and with the rest of the cosmos.

This is why it's important to stay positive and keep your vision clear and pure. Energy information is constantly flowing out from our bodies based on our thoughts and feelings. This is a continuous process. It affects and creates change within the source field and it affects and changes the atoms in the source field.

Everything is really all one thing…light and consciousness. It all conducts the same electromagnetic energy. This information demystifies how things work. It puts us firmly back into the center of our lives and our creative process.

We are not as easily daunted by appearances because we realize that the whole cosmos was created to support and help us. Staying in alignment is up to us and when we are in alignment things always work in our favor by virtue of the energy we are choosing to engage. Knowing this can help us stay on point and inspired.

The entire cosmos is a loving, living, flowing energy field and we relate to it best through our love, focus and intention. The clearer our intention and higher our vibration...the more the field is affected in a positive, conscious way...the more powerful we are in our lives.

God is the consciousness, the light and the love that is present here and a million miles away...in all dimensions and in all circumstances. Everything is happening within the synchronicity of the consciousness of the source field...within the consciousness of God.

Everything is all one thing. And this one thing always has our best interest in mind.

****

<u>I AM UNIFIED WITH, CREATED FROM AND CONNECTED TO THE LOVE AND LIGHT OF THE SOURCEFIELD OF ALL CREATION.</u>

****

<u>Exercise #6</u>

Take time to enjoy yourself out in nature. If possible, take your shoes off and allow your feet to directly touch the earth. Walk alongside natural bodies of water. Touch the leaves. Sit out in the sun. Spending time out in nature allows us to connect to the planet and ground to mother Earth. There is actually a practice called "grounding" or "earthing" that focuses on the vital exchange of electrons that occurs when we are in direct contact with nature.

When we touch the earth with our bare skin or use grounding shoes we absorb the negative electrons flowing up and out from the planet. These negative electrons are vital to the maintenance of our health. As we contact the earth or nature we release positive electrons. This completes the circuit. It's crucial that we release these positive electrons. When they are stored in our bodies they build up and lead to sickness and many other problems. In the same respect, when we absorb negative electrons we rebalance our entire being. This is a part of the cosmic plan for our regeneration and stabilization on the Earth. There are many articles out about grounding / earthing. There is even a documentary about it. Please take time to research and enjoy the many benefits of earthing and purposefully plug yourself back into the cosmic energy that is everywhere.

****

Everything in the cosmos is really all one thing…light. Your consciousness, focus, imagination and intention were created to help you manifest the divine plan of your life out of the light.

CHAPTER 7
UNITY CONSCIOUSNESS

The universal divine energy is constantly moving and expressing through you and every living and inanimate thing on the earth and throughout the cosmos.

Your awareness of this power is the foundation of your own personal power.

The great spiritual teachers of the world have always known that the Divine lived within them and worked through them. The awareness of this connection creates miracles. Divine universal energy is actually the only energy present at all times but what we do with it depends on the level of our consciousness and how committed we are to co-creating the divine plan of our lives.

Source energy connects us to everything. It is non localized, "omnipotent, omnipresent" and aware. It's unconditional love and supreme intelligence. This same energy created all of the worlds as well as all of the flowers and the oceans. It is all knowing and all loving. When we focus on its presence within us a huge energy surge happens in our lives and we begin to walk as the Divine in action. This is how we were intended to live. In this state, we experience our true selves.

The science of successfully manifesting, in ease and grace, lies in aligning with and <u>acknowledging</u> unity consciousness.

The majority of the people on this planet have not yet awakened to the understanding of unity consciousness. They have no clue as to who they are and what they are capable of. Most will live their entire lives without knowing the truth.

When we become conscious of the divine energy within us, our lives change dramatically. Maintaining this awareness is a foundational step in our spiritual growth. It is the secret to growing in our personal power.
Growing in our personal power is as important as growing from a child to an adult.

When we honor unity consciousness everyone and everything becomes important. We seek the highest outcomes for all. We want to be kind and compassionate to others. We choose to be thoughtful and fair.

Every situation ultimately works out in the highest for everyone. If something should go in a direction different than what we thought or hoped for, we can realize that God is inside this new direction even if it was originally perceived as a failure.

It's up to us to stay balanced and move forward taking inspired action no matter how things appear. These kinds of situations usually end up being opportunities that allow us to gain new insights and strengths. The situation may actually turn out to be better than what we had originally intended.

Staying in unity consciousness doesn't mean being a doormat or sacrificing unnecessarily. In fact, it means just the opposite. You may have to hold your boundaries a little stronger. Do it with kindness and compassion. You may find the challenges that come to you not only cause you to move out of your comfort zone but they also heal issues that may have been problematic for you. Every experience comes to help you evolve into your highest and best self.

When opportunities or success comes to us, they come through people the Divine has sent to us. When we help, encourage or support others we are the people the Divine has sent to them. This is about harmony and win/wins for everyone.

Because all of life exists within a huge electromagnetic field if you think about negativity, you will draw negativity to you through the unity of all things. Inversely, if you think about happiness and love you will also draw these things to you through the unity of all things.

When we act in unconditional love, unconditional love acts in us. Everything is functioning within the unity of all things.

When we feel separated from God we are not able to consciously use our power to the fullest. The feeling that we are separated from God leads us to behave in extremely illogical and self-destructive ways. It causes desperation and depression. We become burdened by dogma and conditioning.

We are here to heal the duality and experience of separation in our lives. In the ancient stories humanity was unified with the Divine and then something happened and a fall from Paradise occurred. We were plunged into the illusion that we are separate and alone. We began to experience life cut off from our own power and from love.

When we remove the illusions from our consciousness, we no longer accept the appearances that we are divided, separate from each other and from God. We see everyone and everything as different creative aspects of the Divine and of ourselves. We embrace the unity in all things. We access the power to manifest the life of our dreams faster. We accept and receive God's love for us through all experiences. Healing the illusions of separation allows us to grow into the fullness of our divine potential.

Visualize and experience the oneness of your life with everything and everyone around you. Pray for goodness and healing to express itself in your life and in everyone's life. Get excited about your dreams coming true. Get excited about everyone's beautiful dreams coming true. Seek to do your activities to serve not only yourself but also the highest good of everyone. You will find that all of your needs and wants are abundantly met. You will be a blessing to yourself and all the world.

****

<u>GOD IS USHERING IN HEAVEN ON EARTH THROUGH ME AND THROUGH ALL DIVINE SOULS. I AM ONE WITH ALL OF CREATION.</u>

****

Exercise #7

This is an exercise to expand consciousness.

Pull out your journal. Use your imagination. Take some quiet time and go through these different scenarios pretending and visualizing very deeply.

-Imagine that your goals and dreams are God's goals and dreams. If they have come to you through your intuition, desires and joy then they are. Imagine that the ideas that are coming to you around creating greater happiness are God's ideas for creating greater happiness. How do you feel when you acknowledge that your dreams and goals are being sent to you to from God?

-Imagine that your home is God's home and that your career is God's career. As you acknowledge God's presence and power in your home and career what changes for you? How does the energy shift?

-Imagine that your bank account is God's bank account. Can God have a failing bank account or troubled financial situations? Imagine that as you are acknowledging God's presence in your money and finances that the energy of these things and the energy around and within them completely changes. Write down what you feel and what changes for you.

-Imagine that your friends and loved ones are filled with God's presence and energy. What changes for you when you make this realization? Imagine that the trees and plants around you are all filled with God's presence and power. What do you notice when you spend time with these visualizations? How does bringing your awareness to this change what you feel?

Play with these different scenarios until you can look at all people and situations as being filled with God's energy, love, light and presence. Begin to feel into how this relates to you and how the unity of all things flows through you.

Exercise #7b

Take some quiet time and actively picture and feel the Divine living inside of you. See the energy inside of you. Feel and experience the energy as a great sun shining from your core out into the world. Get a sense of the energy of God moving through you….in and out of your heart...in and out of your lungs. Feel it moving down your arms and legs. Feel it moving through your mind and around your neck, eyes and ears. Feel it moving across your shoulders and down your back and in your stomach. Feel it in your legs, feet and bones. Breathe deeply and bring your awareness to the fact that God has always been in every cell of your body and will always be with you. Remember this. Allow yourself to feel a greater connection to God and everything in your life.

****
You are already connected to everything you could ever want to manifest...including your spiritual awareness, success, health, happiness, abundance and love.

CHAPTER 8
THE SUBCONSCIOUS MIND AND EGO

As mentioned before, the subconscious mind is the aspect of ourselves that holds all of the information we have ever been exposed to or have ever processed. It also holds all of our beliefs and self-created stories. The ego is considered to be an aspect of self that embodies the dominant ideas within the subconscious. For many, it expresses the trauma, frustration and low self-esteem that a person has experienced.

The subconscious mind is like a collection of books within a library. The biofield is actually akin to the building...the library itself, including the shelves and structures that hold all of the books. The ego is the consciousness that springs to life and acts upon the information contained in the books. The ego has an agenda: to inform the individual of all of the pains and traumas that are held in the volumes of "books" of the subconscious mind that haven't been fully processed or integrated. This expression of the ego usually happens in an uncomfortable way that typically involves creating more pain, stress or trauma. The ego expresses the wounding ultimately to bring to light what is present in the subconscious so that the person can witness it, acknowledge the trauma or incoherencies and use the information to create greater healing.

When people are acting in an uncaring or unconscious ways, it is said that their ego is in control. We can look at someone's life respectfully and objectively and see all of the programming and information that is held within their subconscious mind. We see this in how they behave and in what they believe. It's expressed in the way they love themselves and in how they are able to care for themselves and others.

As the subconscious mind stores the information especially specific to trauma, the ego begins to assemble beliefs based on how the information seems to fit together. So if someone was abused and neglected as child as opposed to understanding that their parents or caretaker were at fault and responsible, they may interpret all of this as "I am not getting the love and care I am supposed to be receiving and this is because…I am no good. I don't deserve love. I am not enough. If I were good enough my parents wouldn't have hurt me."

The child's ego creates the belief system based on experiences and acts out on it. "Clearly, I am flawed. I will show the whole world how undeserving I am."

The child usually then begins to act in negative ways towards themselves and others based on these beliefs. This is how the pain of the ego steps in and expresses itself. The individual often times ends up self-sabotaging opportunities without even recognizing that this is what is going on.

In many ways the subconscious/ego seeks to keep a person in a familiar "safe place". This is because the subconscious can deal with the experiences of the "safe place" even though it may not be a very good or healthy place. It's just familiar and manageable.

Today in the world there is a huge surge in the use of manifesting techniques, ie., the law of attraction, visualizations, etc. Many times people find that they do these techniques for a little while with some success but then they ultimately run into blocks. The subconscious and ego prevent people from moving any closer towards their dreams because something about the goal is too threatening and causes resistance or fear.

While the person is doing all of this work on the outer to change the ego may feel:

"Love isn't safe and I don't deserve it."
"Happiness isn't truly available and I don't deserve it."
"Having money is going to make people distance themselves from me and I don't deserve the freedom and options that come from having more of it."

This has been the real problem in manifesting lifestyle changes that I see among my clients. And this is where some of the deepest work lies.

Everyone came to the planet with the same opportunity to excel, succeed and manifest. We have chosen different families to join and different situations in our life to help us evolve and expand into higher levels of creativity and grace.

Regardless of what we go through and however we process it in the moment, if we can remember to love and forgive ourselves unconditionally we will allow ourselves to experience more happiness and joy

When we know that we are deserving of love, and we give this to ourselves, we find the strength to break through any subconscious programming.

The love and acceptance that we are seeking is already inside of us.

****

I AM LOVABLE AND DESERVING OF ALL OF THE GOODNESS GOD WISHES TO BESTOW UPON ME.

THE DIVINE PLAN OF MY LIFE IS POWERFUL. PURSUING IT HEALS AND RESTORES MY SUBCONSCIOUS AND MY LIFE.

****

Exercise #8

This exercise may require more patience, presence and honesty with yourself.

Be gentle with yourself. Take some time and look at the places where you are not loving towards yourself or allowing love in.

Use your journal and make notes.

Look at the places where you are not feeling worthy of goodness in your life. Look at the places where you are not showing yourself kindness and compassion.

Look at the places where you may feel angry or disappointed with yourself. Are there any places where you are punishing yourself or feel bad about yourself?

Write all of these down.

Make a greater effort to show yourself compassion, kindness and love and do the same for all of those you come in contact with.

This is a subtle exercise. It requires expanding your awareness because people have the tendency to convince themselves that they are taking good care of themselves.

Step outside of yourself and take a look at how you treat yourself.

What do you think about yourself? What kind of things do you say to yourself? How do you feel about your life?

There are a lot of modalities geared towards healing the negative patterns in the ego structure. Some of the most successful ones focus on deep forgiveness, kindness, compassion and staying in present moment awareness.

If you can stay focused on your own behavior, you will notice where and when you feel triggered. Being triggered is an automatic reaction as opposed to a response that is based on being compassionate and kind.

As mentioned before, filling the biofield with love and light can also help heal and rebalance the traumatic experiences and imbalances held in the subconscious. I have included a sacred prayer below to help with this. If used regularly it can help in removing the subconscious blocks and conditioning that usually are the cause of people not being able to manifest their highest happiness and their dreams.

****

PRAYER TO REMOVE CONSCIOUS AND SUBCONSCIOUS BLOCKS AND 3RD DIMENSIONAL CONDITIONING

I am of God.
I ground myself to the Earth.

I command you God to remove from my being all conscious and subconscious blocks and 3rd dimensional conditioning, infinite levels high and infinite levels wide, through all past timelines, through all space/time continuum in every dimension.

I command you God to flood all these timelines through all space/time continuum in every dimension with God's divine love.

I thank you God and I send you my unconditional love.
So Be It / Amen

****

*You are a beautiful, divine being worthy of all the best. Be unafraid in showering yourself with happiness, love, joy and success.

CHAPTER 9
THE STARSEEDS

There is a vast and extremely complex sacred matrix that has been created to usher in the divine plan on Earth. At the center of it is the human race. Humanity was created through bringing together many of the starseed races. From each of these races different qualities were chosen and assimilated.

All human souls are precious and holy but the majority of the people who have come to help in the awakening of humanity are from starseed groups. They have come here with a specific purpose. They are working to break through family patterns and societal conditioning in order to transmute them and bring forth a new reality to the planet. There is a myriad of different soul groups that have come to help. They are all playing pivotal roles in the awakening that is currently happening on the planet right now. Because of this, one of the primary ways to manifest the divine plan of your life is to activate your DNA and access the wisdom and assistance of your angelic or starseed family.

If you are reading this, there is a good chance that you are from one of these starseed groups. It is a worthwhile undertaking to connect to your starseed family and get to know them so that you can understand yourself better. The starseeds are all different and each group offers a specific vibration and has emerged from a different dimension. If you are a starseed, the essence of your soul emerged from one of these groups. Finding out more about this is a huge step in your evolution and personal development.

There is a lot that has been forgotten in our world today especially in reference to our divine origins. Connecting with the group that your soul and consciousness emerged from will provide you with a lot of answers and support. Your manifesting power will take an amplified step up. You will access more of your divine power and you will have a starseed family to connect to, learn from and heal with. You'll have a new support group to relate to and grow with. This one thing can change your life dramatically.

If you feel that you are not from a starseed group, please go into meditation and ask God to put a portal around you from the ultimate dimension or the dimension your soul originated from. Pray to God to download your gifts to you and any additional information that is important for you to know. Ask to be connected with the divine angels from the dimension that your soul originated from.

Regardless of where your soul originated from, it's important to connect with the energy and information from that dimension. This will assist you in your spiritual evolution and increase your self-love, personal power, self-knowledge and frequency.

****

I AM CREATED FROM THE STARS, THE HEAVENS AND THE EARTH. MY CAPACITY TO CREATE GOOD FOR MYSELF AND OTHERS IS UNLIMITED.

****

Exercise #9

RECONNECTING TO YOUR STARSEED FAMILY

Starseeds carry the DNA of:

Pleiadians

Arcturians

Sumerians

Atlantarians

Andromedans

Crystal Lumerians

Ashtarians

Sirians, etc.

The way to find out where you are from is as follows. If you feel you are a starseed use your intuition and ask:

Am I Pleiadian? Arcturian? Sumerian? Atlantarian? Andromedan? etc.,....

Wherever you are from, ask God to open a portal to that dimension and to put the other end of the portal around you. Meditate through that dimension, asking God to help you receive information. Your starseed family will download the information and your gifts as you connect to them.

Again, if you feel you are not a starseed, ask God to connect you with the dimension your soul originated from so that information can come to you from that specific dimension. Request that the angels from that dimension come to you to help you on your spiritual journey.

****

Your soul was created to express the beauty and love of the Divine. Enjoy and embrace the experience as a way to get to know yourself better. Enjoy, explore and fulfill the divine plan of your life.

PART II

DIVINE ALIGNMENT

CHAPTER 10
THE DIVINE PLAN /
DIVINE ALIGNMENT

God has created a divine plan for you and every person on the planet.

This plan is co-creative and exists so that you and God can share and experience life together and so that you can have the best life possible. The divine plan is restorative and assists us in keeping our frequency high. It helps us evolve so that we can comprehend the truth of who and what we are and live as the divine beings that we were created to be. Many times because of dogma and conditioning we have a perception of God as being distant, judgmental and unconcerned, but none of this is true. God loves each and every one of us completely and wants us to be happy, healthy, fulfilled and successful.

The divine plan encompasses every area of life… our career, love, abundance, relationships, health and our homes. It graces every experience we could ever have. It's not an end result, it's a journey….and we gain access to this journey through staying in divine alignment.

In turn, divine alignment is accessed through consistently setting your intention, following your intuition/guidance, keeping your frequency high and staying surrendered. Alignment is a process that requires daily action. Each step forward changes and rearranges things. Each step forward requires us to rebalance and make adjustments as we move further into our alignment.

As mentioned before, God's plan for your life contains only your highest happiness, success and abundance. One might ask if there is a divine plan for everyone, why more people on the planet are not experiencing it? The answer is simple. People have lost the knowledge of God's plan. The majority of people don't have an active committed relationship with God and therefore they don't know all of the goodness that God has created for them. They can't see it and so they don't act on it. It's like looking for a particular address and passing it on the street without realizing it. All the same if you want to find the address you are going to have to keep looking for it until you find it. The responsibility of creating alignment lies within each individual.

It's as though there has been some form of collective amnesia around the divine plan and divine alignment. And because this absence of knowledge spans down through eons of time and down through countless generations, people have been conditioned for thousands of years to believe that life is difficult and without Grace. The predominant societal structures on the planet are ones that generate and sustain problems. There haven't been any consistent sources of information that have truly taught us that we are divine and that happiness is our birthright and within our reach.

We are God's children and God wants goodness to fill our lives, in the same way that a healthy parent only wants goodness for their child. But if we, for whatever reason, don't step forward and claim it, we may go without ever experiencing it in our lives. It's up to each one of us to say yes to it, invest in it and birth it into the physical.

Be willing to stay connected to Source energy and have an active relationship with the Divine. This alone will provide enough energy to help you stay focused and motivated to take daily steps in order to stay in alignment and on track with the goals and dreams you are seeking to manifest.

Be willing to feel God, embrace God and surrender to the divine plan…outside of any dogma, religious programming or conditioning you may have experienced.

The divine plan creates happiness, vibrant health, peace, joyous experiences, loving relationships, abundance and success in all areas of your life. It creates good feelings and causes a person to constantly evolve into better versions of themselves. It assists a person in truly knowing themselves as a creator and child of God. It brings all the aspects of a person's life together in complete harmony and balance.

If every person alive today were living the divine plan for their lives, our beautiful Earth would be a very different place. Life would be harmonious.

The divine plan connects everyone's life together in a compatible, cooperative and harmonious way. Everyone naturally has different likes and dislikes, joys and passions. The divine makes use of synchronicity and alignment to build upon the universal blueprint for the planet where everyone is acknowledged and honored. If we were all aligned with the divine plan, there would be boundless creativity and loving expressions everywhere. There would be absolutely no competition or failure in a traditional sense, because within the divine plan there is more than enough for everyone.

The idea of competition doesn't exist within the divine plan because all have been amply provided for.

Within this plan each one of us has an incredible journey to experience. We know what the aspects of this plan are when we look at the things in our lives that make us the happiest. What would we love to be doing if money wasn't a consideration? Where and how would we love to live? What kinds of ways would we love to honor our physical bodies in terms of exercise, movement or meditation? How would we enjoy helping the planet become a better place?

Many times people have a passion or a dream to do something but they allow themselves to be discouraged or talked out of it by other people or by the idea that they can't make enough money doing it. If it truly is part of the divine plan for your life, you will be amply provided for. Instead of thinking you can't make money this way, remember all of the people who have been successful doing the same thing. If they can do it so can you.

When we do something that we love and we acknowledge the joy and happiness it brings us we open ourselves up to receive more happiness and joy. Being continuously successful and joyous is a concept that we must embrace and be willing to allow into our lives. Feeling joyous is God's way of letting you know you are on the right path and are doing the right thing.

When you are in divine alignment living the divine plan for your life, using your divine gift, abundance and money will flow. When you are not in alignment money may be difficult to obtain and your life typically won't have the same levels of joy. In fact, it may be difficult, stressful, tedious, and unsatisfying.

When I was not in alignment, money was scarce and my life was difficult and stressful. I was actually manifesting "lack of" as opposed to the life God had for me. I had a choice in this and although I didn't completely understand it at the time, I was out of alignment. Of course it wasn't intentional, all the same I was participating in creating the problems.

When I stepped into alignment with the divine plan for my life, abundance started to flow, situations became easier and opportunities for me to share my gifts and be abundantly compensated, grew. When we are in alignment, we are living our life's passion and using our gifts to help ourselves and the world. When we are out of alignment, life has more challenges. We experience more stress and we are not as happy.

One way to know if you are in alignment or not is to gauge how happy and fulfilled you are and how abundant your resources are.

If there is an area of your life where you are experiencing lack, you may want to take a closer look at your choices and where you are placing your focus.

We have been conditioned into scarcity, into living with "less than" and into "lack of" in many areas of our lives.

God didn't create scarcity and poverty, we did, through practicing and engaging in negative thoughts, emotions and behaviors.

God created unbounded abundance and joy. Just take a look at the abundance of nature. Fruit trees give abundantly. Flowers bloom in all kinds of variety and color across the planet endlessly. The oceans, seashores and trees are filled with so much abundance that you can't keep track of it all.

Abundance is our birthright. It is the divine intention that abundance flow joyously through every aspect of our lives.

Knowing this…. truly believing and experiencing this... allows us to release our doubts and fears. We experience a very close and loving relationship with ourselves and our creator. We feel deserving of and grateful for the divine plan. We allow ourselves to receive God's goodness and we stay in alignment with greater ease and grace. We transform who we are and how we live. We begin to see ourselves in a different light. We become more than what we can currently imagine. The divine energy and power within us expands and we begin to live as God intended.

Life becomes a wonderful, beautiful journey and we manifest our portion of Heaven on Earth.

****

<u>DIVINE ALIGNMENT BRINGS JOY, LOVE, PROSPERITY, ABUNDANCE, SUCCESS AND MIRACLES INTO MY LIFE. THE DIVINE PLAN FOR MY LIFE USHERS IN MY DIVINE BIRTHRIGHT.</u>

****

Exercise #10

Take out your journal. Work with the following ideas -

Look back over your life. Look at the different experiences that you've had where you were clearly in divine alignment, following your guidance and moving in the direction of your highest good. See how these experiences connected together and brought you forward in joy and fulfillment.

Now look at other experiences where you may have felt that you were not in alignment, either not at all or to the extent that you wished you were. Note these experiences. When you look at these experiences where you weren't in alignment you can also see a pattern where an education was gained and you understood in hindsight how to stay in alignment better.

If you have any regrets, forgive yourself and send yourself unconditional love. You did the best you knew at the time and it's important to love and honor yourself and where you have been in your journey.

You can send love as easily into the past thereby shifting the timeline as you can send it into the future. Sending love into the future can also be considered a form of prayer. In the same respect you can send love into the past to yourself to heal and create more positivity around situations where you feel you weren't in the highest alignment.

Take some time with each incident where you were in alignment and where you were out of alignment. Breathe deeply and send yourself love through all of those experiences…noting the difference in how it feels to send yourself love when you were in alignment and noting how it feels when you send yourself love in the experiences where you were out of alignment. Breathe and send love. Breathe and send love. Process any emotions that may come up. Remember that all of the experiences you've had allowed you to gain an education and that sending love and forgiving yourself surrounds you with love and shifts the frequency of the experience.

Exercise #10b

Look at what you feel is working in your life and what isn't working.

Look at the areas in your life where you are experiencing difficulties, if any.

Are there any commonalities in these areas?

Look at the emotions that you are experiencing in the areas where there may be difficulties.

Take time out and go into a quiet space within. Ask your higher self how you can bring about greater levels of divine alignment in your life. Ask yourself what life would look like if you were in alignment in all areas in your life? How would it feel and how would things be different? Allow the ideas to flow to you to bring about the highest forms of alignment on a daily basis.

Take the steps to create greater alignment. Eventually the challenges and difficulties will shift and life will get easier and more enjoyable as you continue to move into greater levels of balance and alignment.

****

Step into the Divine Plan of your life. Step into Alignment.

CHAPTER 11
DISCOVERING AND
USING YOUR GIFTS

Everyone came to the planet with a special set of gifts to help them manifest the divine plan. Through using them in our personal lives and in our careers, we access greater alignment and we evolve.

Using our gifts involves embracing our creativity. Unfortunately, many of us have lost the wisdom of what creativity is. Creativity is God's vision and presence. It comes to us through inspiration which comes to us directly from our soul/higher self and the Divine. Through embracing creativity and inspiration, we immerse ourselves in God's love and energy. We come to understand the different stages of alignment and we create beauty and balance in all areas of our lives.

Our gifts, no matter what they are, spring forth through creativity.

Everyone's gifts are different and everyone's gifts are designed to work in harmony with one another. We gain a myriad of benefits from using our gifts. They fill us with happiness, energy, enthusiasm and positive vibrations. Sickness and imbalance are less frequent. We grow. We expand. We feel more connected to God and to our purpose.

Once we dedicate our lives to using our gifts our lives change dramatically.

My gifts brought me out of one lifestyle and into another. They brought me out of one country and into another. They took me from a place where I was living out of the back of my car to a place where I am helping thousands of people Internationally in a thriving, satisfying career. All of this was a process, however. I had to change a lot. I invested a tremendous amount time and effort in order to be able to master and use my gifts.

When I found myself homeless, I got on public assistance and started looking for a job. I responded to all kinds of job listings...everything from bartending to cleaning. No one would hire me. The more I looked for a job, the less I was able to get a job.

I asked God what was going on and the response I got in my Spirit was that I wasn't able to get a job because I wasn't supposed to get a job. I was supposed to meditate. Because I was on public assistance, I could do this. I was specifically being asked by the Divine to stop everything in my life and meditate for hours at a time every day for 4 years.

And so that's what I did.

God knew that in order for me to be able to use my gifts I needed to have a complete overhaul in my consciousness and energy field. I was committed and dedicated to this process and at the end of the four years I emerged and began the healings that I am now doing through my ministry.

The changes that you will have to make in order to use your gifts most likely won't be as extreme as the ones I had to make. All the same, they may require courage, dedication, perseverance and a willingness to grow in order to see the whole process through.

In retrospect, I can say that investing the time and energy that it took to develop and understand my gifts was one of the most worthwhile things I have ever done. I have a wonderful life now. I am living on purpose. I know for a fact that I am living the life that God intended for me and I live in a constant state of gratitude. I am in service and I am abundantly provided for. Every day the way I use my gifts changes and evolves. I love being continuously surprised by the direction my life takes. I enjoy how it always brings me closer to God.

I wouldn't be the person I am today and I wouldn't be able to help people and serve in the way I do if I hadn't evolved along this path. The journey has been remarkable and invaluable. I had to constantly take action not always knowing exactly where it would lead me.

I only knew I was supposed to use my gifts.
I surrendered to this.

Had I continued to seek jobs once I had gotten the information that I was supposed to meditate, I can't say what would have happened. But I do know that I would have clearly stepped out of alignment and I doubt that I would have reached the place that I am now. In fact, I am sure things would have gotten worse. It took a lot of courage and determination to exclusively meditate. At the time I didn't see all of the benefits that I was gaining from this. In hindsight, it's obvious.

I was able to raise my frequency dramatically and information, techniques and processes were downloaded to me that I would need in order to help people. I became a different person. I opened myself up to new situations and opportunities. Everything in my life today has evolved from this sacrifice and dedication. It took years of learning, practicing and development in order to reach the place where I was capable of using my gifts to my highest potential. I had to really apply myself in order for this happen.

If you don't know what your gifts are, spend the time and effort needed to discover them. It's that important. It is central to developing your connection to the Divine and to maintaining alignment.

Your gifts are connected to your dreams and your desires. And your dreams and desires are unique to you and are manifested through using your gifts.

Your dreams and desires are a gift from God. They were put into your heart so that you could experience the highest states of joy and fulfillment. And because God gave you your gifts this means that your capacity to manifest them was also given to you.

Put another way, because you were born with your gifts, you were born to manifest your gifts. The way to do this already exists. Firmly knowing and believing this helps you to move forward with greater confidence.

The culture that we live in today has totally minimized the idea that we can live in a continuously joyous state. This is not "the normal" that is promoted. Granted, life is very stressful for many people, but in all due respect, the majority of stress is ultimately the result of living outside of alignment.

In addition, the ideas that are popularized in society are ones where only a few people have all of the things that everyone else "should" want and these few only do certain occupations. All of this makes it seem like there are only certain occupations or careers that are really fulfilling or enjoyable. This is just what's promoted. It's not the truth.

Everyone enjoys different things and has a different dream in their heart. It's important to find what really makes your heart sing.

If you don't already know what your gifts are ask the Divine for assistance to help you understand your dreams, deepest desires and your gifts. These three things work together. They are brought to you through the energy of your soul and they are connected to your purpose. I have included a special sacred prayer at the end of this chapter that you can use to help you in this process.

What do you get the most joy from doing? What are you good at? What would you love to do if you could make more than enough money to support yourself, your family and all of your projects?

Do you love teaching or organic farming?
Do you love painting, sculpting or helping people reach their goals?
What about writing, home making, landscaping or working with animals?
Do you love to act, design beautiful living spaces or create websites? Do you love numbers or politics? What about research or science?
Perhaps making music or preparing foods for friends and family makes your heart happy. Maybe you love hiking or helping people heal.

Discovering and using your gifts to manifest your dreams shifts your focus in your life and ushers in high levels of divine energy. It raises your personal vibration and the vibration of the planet. You enjoy happier, healthier friendships and your contribution to the world accelerates.

After surrendering on a daily basis to the Divine, using my gifts is one of the most important things I commit to. God gave them to me for the purpose of putting them into use and extending the divine vision into world. The Divine supports you when you use your gifts. You will absolutely be successful and abundantly provided for. How can it be any other way? God is creating this through you.

At the same time, the process of embracing and bringing your gifts out into the world may cause you to have to face your subconscious beliefs and change them. I have found that doing what it takes to develop and use your gifts is often the very thing that was needed to create a balanced life and heal deep seated patterns. Making the shift into embracing your gifts is not always the easiest thing to pursue but it is always the best thing. They hold a huge piece of your individual essence. It is uniquely your own work and allowing yourself to break through any blocks or resistance that you may have to doing this work is one of the most worthwhile things you could ever do. You can choose to view this as a wonderful thing…like "Wow!!! Look at what I get to do!! How wonderful!!"

Allow yourself to heal and release any fear or stress that you may have around using your gifts. Cultivate a supportive, optimistic attitude that will assist you in having and pursuing your highest happiness. Take consistent steps towards using your gifts and maintain an attitude of preparedness.

When we resist using our gifts we are out of alignment. Doing this creates a dysfunctional cycle because the more you resist your gifts the more difficult life becomes and the more you have to work at other jobs to survive. Whereas the more you use your gifts, the less drudgery there is in your life and the more joyous, satisfying and prosperous your experience is. You thrive.

For some, it might seem like a daunting, courageous and perhaps even overly stressful thing to pursue a life filled with your dreams and passions, especially if this is a new idea to you. It's counter culture when there is so much out there about dreams not coming true and not being able to have all you desire. But again, this is all conditioning. It's not true.

Your specific contribution has been created and given to you by God. The whole world needs the specific contribution that you have come here to make and you are deeply valued. Realizing and honoring the sacredness and importance of your life can be huge in terms of finding the inner strength and self-esteem to pursue your dreams. Your contribution is uniquely your own and no one could ever take your place or do what you came to do in the way that you can do it.

You are unique in all the world and in the divine plan.

And so, as mentioned before, remembering that because God gave you these dreams that you were also given, the way to make them manifest and serve through them may be helpful to you in strengthening your resolve. You just may not understand the whole picture yet, but it does exist already. You don't have to struggle with this and figure it out. The universe has already organized all of this. All you have to do is get quiet and allow the Divine to bring the "how's" of it all to you through inspiration. Be willing to fully believe in yourself and in the contribution that you have come here to make.

Align your thoughts and feelings with the understanding that God is creating through you when you use your gifts. Remember that your ideas and dreams are not too good to be true or too wonderful to manifest. If we think these things, we are working against ourselves. Our lives are supposed to be wonderful and amazing. We need more of this on the planet.

Once you make up your mind to follow your path using your gifts, stay committed. I had to stay extremely committed through various scenarios. In time, with consistent effort and persistence my life changed. You may face challenges in pursuing your gifts. Embrace them and work through them. They will teach you things you need to know to create your life more completely. Everyday rededicate yourself to using your gifts. They will allow you to express more of yourself and more of the Divine in your life and in the world. They will help you create a more fulfilling and happier life than any other path you could take. You will be amply rewarded, financially and in other ways too.

Dare to dream courageously. You do not have to know how it will manifest. All you have to do is surrender and let God bring it to you. Your responsibility is to follow your intuitive leads, take action and allow the joy, happiness and abundance to build. Open and expand yourself so that you can hold more and more positive energy. This will allow you to receive the gifts from all of your work... be it money, gratitude from others, a more satisfying life or more happiness.

In using your gifts, you evolve into the greatest version of yourself. You help others to have a better life and you inspire them to understand that the life that they have been dreaming of is possible.

You usher in the highest frequencies to the planet. You bask in the presence of the Divine flowing through you as your gifts flow out into the world. What a wonderful experience.

****

<u>I USE MY GIFTS TO CREATE HAPPINESS FOR MYSELF AND OTHERS. I ALLOW MYSELF TO DO WHAT I LOVE TO DO.</u>

****

<u>Exercise #11</u>

Think about the things that you love to do...that give you energy and joy. Use your journal and list your ideas.

Create the list specifically to get a sense of what your gifts might be if you don't already know.

Pick the top things on your list and think about how other people have created successful careers around these same activities. Imagine yourself doing these things and living an abundant, joyous life from doing them. Daydream. Allow the joy to build as you do this.

Make yourself a gratitude list where you are giving thanks for the opportunity to do these things while being well compensated. Saying thank you in advance for your gifts and for your dreams creates a powerful conduit to them and helps to bring them in faster.

Make a daily effort to use and expand your gifts. Create opportunities where you can serve through using your gifts and be joyously compensated in doing so.

Set your intention daily to use your gifts. Actively engage in your gifts and in sharing them with people.

Take time to say a prayer that everyone on Earth find and use their gifts and that the joy, happiness, love and abundance that is generated through this, heal the entire planet.

****

<u>LIFE PURPOSE PRAYER</u>

I am of God.
I ground myself to the Earth.

I command you God to give me direction as to my highest life purpose and to help me fulfill this purpose swiftly, effectively and for the good of all concerned.

I command you to infuse me with the energy, strength and inspiration needed to fulfill this mission.

I thank you God and send you my unconditional love.
So Be It / Amen

****
*Using your gifts will completely transform
your life and the planet.*

CHAPTER 12
THE ART OF CONSCIOUSLY MANIFESTING / GIVING AND RECEIVING

The act of manifesting is based on giving and receiving. It follows all of the natural processes in the world and in our bodies.

We breathe in and out. Oxygen enters into our body, circulates, revitalizes and then we breathe out carbon dioxide. Our hearts beat, blood pulses into the heart and then out into the body.

Our minds receive inspired ideas from the divine and then we release these ideas into the world where we use them to create.

This same process also holds true for maintaining alignment and manifesting your dreams.

We receive into our lives based on what we give out.

As mentioned earlier, our thoughts, feelings and behaviors send out vibrations into the world and these vibrations return to us clothed in their corresponding material forms as the experiences, people and situations that make up our lives.

The universe responds to those things we focus on and the frequencies we hold...and arranges all kinds of synchronicities, opportunities, coincidences and "seemingly random" meetings with people to help us fulfill our desires and goals.

It's all extremely impersonal and precise. It's like clockwork in how it all plays out. And yet it's also very personal in the way it affects us directly and shapes our life.

A person who is constantly angry is sending out angry energy into the universe and receiving back the vibrational match of what she/he is sending out. This person's life will most typically be harder and their experiences will usually involve more pain or trauma. They will find their belief systems supported by experiences that lead them to believe that life is hard and unfair and that they are justified in feeling angry. They will find more than enough evidence to support this.

In the same respect, a person who has a positive outlook towards life, who is constantly finding something to be grateful for and who is able to show kindness and compassion to others will experience the world in a completely different way. This person is releasing high frequency vibrations into the universe. In return they will attract positive experiences, happier people, enjoyable relationships and joyous opportunities in life. It's very simple. Like attracts like.

We can always change our outer experiences by changing what we are offering to the universe. Choose to offer positive energy and unconditional love. Choose to increase the joy in your life and in the lives of others. Choose to align with unconditional love. Choose to allow it. Bring your best you forward. This will bring you into alignment with happiness, fulfillment and abundance.

Decide that you will not create any problems for yourself or anyone else. Decide that you will only create based on joy and alignment. Decide that you will approach all others with integrity, kindness and compassion.

The more you acknowledge the Divine in yourself and in your life, the more the divine essence will show up for you to experience. Walk in gratitude and in appreciation. Focus on goodness and goodness will expand. Honor yourself and others in all you do.

Look at the things in your life that are working….and look at the things within your life that are not working. All of this, the good and the undesirable, has come into place because of the mix of frequencies you are offering to the universe.

And so, in spite of the fact that we are divine beings and that God only wants the best for us should we choose something else outside of our divine birthright…..this is what we will create through the vibration and frequency we send out.

God wants to honor your process as a creator and will not interfere unless asked.

Most of us want to receive things in order to ultimately experience happiness. We want the car, the house, perfect health, abundance, amazing relationships all to experience a greater sense of happiness. In the same respect, happiness is an integral part of our divine birthright.

Because of this, one of the most important things we can ever do is choose to be happy right now.

No matter how things look or feel, going into deep acceptance and gratitude allows us to change what we are offering to the world. In this way we break the cycle and raise our frequency.

Choose to be happy and grateful right now. We can't wait for things to come along to generate happiness within us. Ultimately we need to choose to be happy first in order to create and sustain happiness in the long run.

Some people are afraid of getting too happy and they self-sabotage themselves. This conveniently reinforces the notion that dreams don't come true and that life is a constant struggle. If this is something that you've had a problem with or if you know someone who is afraid of being happy, you may want to consider doing the "Melchizedek Meditation" in addition to the "24 heart Chakra Release Meditation" daily. These can be found on our meditation app.

They will assist in clearing the energy blockages and stuck patterns that usually are present when people have difficulty manifesting sustained levels of joy and happiness.

Life is about expansion and growth. We can see this everywhere in nature. We are creating and changing with every breath. With every breath we can align with the divine plan.

As you offer goodness, you allow the Divine within you to flow out to the universe. As you open to receive, you allow the goodness that is the divine plan in the world to reach you.

****

I AM RESPONSIBLE FOR WHAT HAPPENS IN MY LIFE. I RECEIVE BASED ON WHAT I GIVE. I CHOOSE TO OFFER JOY, UNCONDITIONAL LOVE, GRATITUDE AND PEACE.

****

Exercise #12

WORKING WITH GRATITUDE

Use your journal for this.

Find a quiet place where you can contemplate different aspects of your life.

Begin to go over all of the things in your life that are working. Truly feel gratitude for each one of them. Try to spend at least fifteen minutes a day doing this.

You can make a list in the morning as you are waking up of things that you are grateful for. Try to list at least 10 things daily.

When you are doing this seek to stay as present as possible and allow the feelings of gratitude to really sink in. Most people have more positive things going on in their lives than they allow themselves to be aware of.

Allow the feelings to go deep inside. Quietly say "thank you" for all that has gone well...say and feel the words "thank you" deeply from you heart.

Try to stay in the emotion and feeling of gratitude throughout the day. As you continue this practice you will find that you have more and more to be grateful for and you will notice a marked difference in your frequency and vibration. This in turn will bring in more and more experiences that will match your new frequency. This one activity of staying in gratitude throughout the day will transform your life.

Take time to write down all you are grateful for every day. As you grow your gratitude list, you will constantly notice more things to be grateful for. You will witness how important perception in. We choose what we focus on and what we focus on amplifies.

Actively picture wonderful things happening for those you love and those around you. Wishing others well, will shower them with abundance and joy. In return the universe will shower you with more abundance and joy.

Exercise #12b

Take your giving into the physical.
The more you give in the physical the more you open yourself up in the physical to receive.

Look at different ways that you can exert your giving power.

Find causes that you can donate to on a monthly basis.
Surprise loved ones with things you know have value to them.

Increase your reach with what you are willing to give in order to help someone else.

Give your time, energy and ideas in order to help.

Look at all of the ways you are willing to give that feel right to you.
Initially you may have to stretch in order to this but it will become a habit that will allow you to increase your capacity to hold and distribute kindness and abundance.

****
Create Consciously. Dream Positively and Vividly. Choose happiness. Choose love. Choose To Give And Receive Only The Best.

CHAPTER 13
BELIEFS AND SELF-CREATED STORIES

Everyone has a set of beliefs and a story they tell about themselves and their world. Our beliefs form the foundation of our perceptions. It's through these beliefs that we take action and create the world around us. They impact how and why we make choices. Some people's beliefs are positive. Out of this they are able to create greatness and beauty in the world. Many people's beliefs are negative and self-destructive. They are filled with low self-esteem, lack of trust and violence. They create imbalance in the person and in the world.

The story we tell ourselves is how we see our self. It describes how we feel we are being treated...what we feel we deserve...how we perceive the world, how we perceive ourselves and... how we believe things to be.

It's the… "Everything always works out" or the "life is not fair". It's the… "Relationships are wonderful." ...or ... "Relationships are painful".

It's the... "I'm not enough. Nothing ever works for me.", "Life is hard.", "You have to work hard.", etc.

It's also the... "The universe supports me in everything!!", "This is going to be a great day!", "I am so excited to work with people who think the way I do!", "Loving relationships are at the center of my life! I am so grateful for all of the people I know and love."

What you believe and tell yourself is up to you.

Most of us are on automatic with our stories and belief systems. They continuously run through our minds, limiting or expanding what we allow ourselves to experience. They project outwards and the universe is responding to them...good or bad, true or false, helpful or destructive...or anywhere in between.

We always have a choice in how we feel about ourselves and the stories we make up. And ultimately, they are only stories. We have created them and given them value. We don't even recognize that the majority of the time they aren't even real. But we cling to them because the subconscious uses them to keep us safe from whatever we unconsciously believe can harm us.

In other words, we may have negative beliefs around love relationships...not because of what they are but because we fear being hurt or rejected. We may have fear over success or fear of failure and sabotage our opportunities.

Sometimes people have limiting beliefs in all areas of their lives. They don't even recognize this but they end up living boxed in and closed off from their dreams, not because of what is true but because of what they are afraid of and believe.

These stories are the scripts which dictate how our lives run. They color our feelings and behaviors and they create patterns. As we allow ourselves to be controlled and triggered by these patterns, we end up many times creating the very things we say we don't want.

It's important to be able to see and understand our beliefs. We have to put the time in to investigate, understand and free ourselves from our stories if they are not creating positive experiences.

We may be seeking to have certain experiences in our lives but these core patterns and beliefs are expressing the exact opposite. Interestingly enough, we can view this as a blessing because they are showing us where we are out of alignment. They are showing us the exact places where we need to work on ourselves. When we can take an honest look at our lives and what we need to change within our consciousness we can begin to move forward and intentionally change our story to one we enjoy.

If we don't understand what our patterns or beliefs are, we can gain insight into what we believe by taking a look at what is going on in our lives.

If we have problems with relationships, we can assume we have negative beliefs and stories about relationships. If we have problems with being successful, we can assume we have negative beliefs in this area also.

If we are experiencing financial problems, we can assume that we have negative beliefs around money and what it means to be financially abundant.

Down through generations people have been disenfranchised and have come to believe that money is bad and that those who have it are cruel and untrustworthy. We can see that part of this is coming from within the group consciousness because so many people are experiencing the same idea. People have felt undeserving. They have felt incapable of generating and sustaining wealth. They have felt like their dreams can't come true. In many cases they have felt like goodness will come to other people but not to them.

People have been conditioned to believe that love equals pain and that love relationships are intrinsically flawed. They have been conditioned to believe that life is hard and that they have to toil and struggle in order to survive.

Much of what we believe has been influenced by outside sources. We inherit a lot of our beliefs from our parents and our families. Sometimes we inherit beliefs from our culture or the group collective. In some cases, we even inherit beliefs and stories from past lives. These can be more difficult to discern because we may have no working memory of what caused the belief.

Regardless of where our beliefs have come from, it's important to do the inner work. Forgive yourself and those in your world who have helped shape your beliefs and stories. Ask God and your higher self to reveal to you what beliefs need to be healed in the areas where you face challenges. Make the effort to do the inner work.

As you are working through this process you may want to take a look at how your parents and family felt about money, success or relationships. Are there any similarities to your beliefs? Do you spend money in the same way as they do? Are your finances at the same level as your parents?

Most people have been conditioned to believe in fear, debt and problems. They have been conditioned to focus on what they do not want and in doing this they create more resistance and problems.

Many people focus on and remember the situations in their lives where things didn't go well. This keeps the energy of these situations alive and reproducing the energetic patterns of the negative experience. So you may not be experiencing the exact same kinds of situations continuously but you most likely will be experiencing situations that continue to bring up the same kinds of negative emotions, drama and lack. If you dwell on past memories where things didn't go well you will continue to manifest the essence of things not going well in your future.

Begin to look at your past differently. Start pulling out memories where things went well. Be willing to change how you see yourself. Tell yourself a positive story in order to attract more happiness and joy. Create beliefs and stories around goodness and the goodness will expand.

If you dwell on past mistakes, be willing to release this behavior. Don't blame yourself for your past choices. Understand that you did the best you knew how with what you were working through at the time. Forgive yourself, love yourself and send positive energy back to yourself in the past. When you forgive and love your past… and your past self…you change the energetic dynamic and you make room to create a new future with greater progress. You may not like who you were being at the time but if you choose a different perspective, allow yourself to receive the gifts from the experience and gain an education from it, you will move forward with forgiveness, inner peace and self-love.

Take responsibility for your past actions. Sending love into the past and to all involved will shift the energy around what happened and allow you to experience more positivity now. If you need to make amends or fix a situation where you caused a problem by all means do what you are led to do. Let this free you to be at peace.

The past that we remember has been filtered through our perceptions and interpretations. When we are willing to take another look at negative things that have happened and send love and forgive, we release ourselves from self-judgment, guilt and blame. We emerge freer and stronger. We are able to sustain higher and higher frequencies and stay in divine alignment more often.

In order to create something different in your life it's important to change your beliefs about what you think is possible for you to experience.

Reconstruct a whole new version of your past based on what did go right and the strengths you found even in the midst of difficulty. List the strengths that you do have and allow yourself to see the positives in your journey. Bless yourself for the good choices you did make or the education that you gained. Let this help you form a belief that you can achieve your dreams. Look at all of the people who have succeeded in areas that you are seeking success, for example relationships, careers, lifestyle. Become determined and know that if they can do it you can too. What kinds of things would they have to believe in order to have created the life that they did? If nothing else, they would have to believe that their success was possible and that they were worthy of it and deserved it. Remember the instances in your past where you were a success. Noticing and being grateful for your past successes will help you to create more success in the present and in the future.

Monitor your beliefs and stories carefully. They are influencing what you are manifesting. Tell yourself wonderful stories about yourself. Believe that it is possible for you to experience success in every area of your life. Start by viewing yourself as a success now.

Work diligently to believe only the best about yourself and the best in life will present itself to you.

****

<u>MY BELIEFS SHAPE MY WORLD. I BELIEVE I AM SO SPECIAL AND DESERVE THE BEST IN EVERY AREA OF MY LIFE.</u>

****

<u>Exercise #13</u>

Using your journal write out an accurate description of what is going on in your life.

Write out what is working and what isn't working.
Make your list as descriptive and as thorough as possible.

Make a list of beliefs that would have to be present in order to create the different aspects of your life where things are working and where things aren't working.

Where you have found negative beliefs, imagine a positive belief in its place that would support you.

Write out the aspects of your story that keep you trapped and in a limited perspective and experience.

Once you have thoroughly written down all that you can, go into go into a quiet place within and offer all of your stories and belief systems up to God. Ask God to help you in transmuting all of your issues and belief systems. Fully surrender it all to God.

Begin to count the blessings in your story. Remember the positives. See where you have allowed yourself to grow in spite of any setbacks. Recognize how you have been able to make progress in life.

If you feel led, download our meditation and prayer app and use them as daily tools to help you transmute your feelings and belief systems.

There is a lot of information online about releasing limiting beliefs. You may also want to seek the help of a skilled energy practitioner or join one of our online healing groups.

****

Believe in your greatness. Believe in the power of God within you to create goodness and fulfilling experiences in your world. This is the true source of your power, your happiness and your abundance.

CHAPTER 14
NEGATIVE INFLUENCES

There can be various negative influences in a person's life which cause them to unknowingly manifest situations and outcomes they don't want. There is a huge mechanism playing out behind the scenes that is connected to the negativity and violence found on the planet. This same mechanism is connected to the destructive aspects of consumerism. These negative influences are virtually invisible to most people and yet they are creating the vast majority of the problems found in our world today. In some cases, a person's entire life is influenced by these negative forces and yet they may never know that they are being affected, used, violated and manipulated.

It's an unfortunate truth that there are those who would make a conscious effort to cause harm to others. This is something we should face honestly so that we can make sure we are safe and protected.

People sometimes feel like the manifesting process doesn't work or that something is wrong with them because they're making the effort but they're not able to manifest in the same way that others do.

Everyone has the same capacity and potential to manifest goodness. The truth is that people are being affected by negative influences and their manifesting processes is suffering because of this.

As your consciousness expands, and you commit yourself to staying in divine alignment one of the things that will happen is that you will become aware the negative influences that may be playing out in your life. Being aware of when and how negative influences are playing out in your life will help tremendously because you will be able to sense, address and remedy these influences so that they don't have the same opportunity to violate you and manipulate situations in your life.

Below is a list of the primary negative influences that people face today.

NEGATIVE ENTITIES

One of the biggest negative influences on the planet is negative entities. These entities live in a person's biofield and in a person's body. They can act from different dimensions to create interferences, violations and manipulations in a person's life. They do this in order to drain the life force energy from people and manipulate their lives. Because they are largely invisible to the eye, most people don't know that they are being influenced by outside forces. At the same time, these entities/energies take advantage of people and lock into a person's body and wreak havoc in their lives. They thrive off of negative energy, (anger, pain, violence, depression, anxiety, etc) and they manipulate people into creating negative situations and negative emotions which the entities then feed off of. While most people don't perceive entities with their eyes, they can sense and feel them. There is usually an uneasy feeling or a negative emotional response when one has an entity attachment. A person's life may begin to reflect more negativity or what one might call bad luck. At the same time, there also may not be a marked negative feeling. There might simply be the sense that something isn't quite right.

Many times when someone is suicidal, bipolar, suffering from anxiety, OCD or PTSD there is an entity present.

In the vast majority of cases when people come to me with these symptoms I find an entity present. I remove the entity(s) and help them rebalance their energy. I find that the presence of entities is so common that most people have some form of entity or energetic attachment without knowing that it's there. Because of this I have included an entity/energetic attachment removal as a standard procedure in all of my protocols when working with people.

If you feel you have an entity/energetic attachment or if you feel you know someone who does, please don't hesitate to get help from a skilled practitioner or get on one of our group calls so that you can have these attachments removed and your energetic field and body cleared and rebalanced.

I have also created a prayer to remove an entity from a person's body. It can be found on our prayer app. It has also been included in the rear of this book and at the end of this chapter.

NEGATIVE REMOTE VIEWERS

Negative remote viewers are beings/people who are viewing you and your life from another place or dimension. These beings are monitoring you in order to gather information, manipulate/violate you, create irritation, wreak havoc in your life and steal energy. The majority of people on the planet have been intrusively monitored by these beings/people and most governments even teach remote viewing classes in the military for espionage work.

Sometimes people, immediately after waking up, will suddenly feel a sense of anxiety, irritation or fear. This is usually the signal that a remote viewer is present and is sending you negative energy in order to manipulate your emotions and get your day off to a bad start.

You can usually sense the presence of remote viewers. Sometimes there is an uneasy or irritated feeling. You may also feel like something is off. These remote viewers seek to influence your mood and your life in order to lower your frequency and manipulate you into generating negative emotions. They can have a devastating impact on a person's life.

Remote viewing isn't a skill that is limited to a few select people. Anyone can learn how to remote view and if one develops their intuitive skills they may find that remote viewing and intuitively gathering information are not completely dissimilar. In fact, they are very close. Intuition is part of every person's endowment for the sake of receiving information from the Divine and functioning in one's life more effectively. Remote viewing is typically used to manipulate outcomes and harm others. This does not have to be the case and it can be used for good. However, this is not the common use.

I have included sacred prayers at the end of this chapter that will help remove remote viewers.

SPELLS, CURSES, BLACK MAGIC AND ANCIENT RITUALS

Spells, curses, black magic and ancient rituals are incredibly commonplace today. They are used, often times by remote viewers, to harm, manipulate, violate and drain people of energy. They are constructed to target specific situations and to hold people back, causing them to struggle and feel discombobulated. Spells and ancient rituals are the opposite of prayers and sending positive energy. These things can be addressed and removed. Consider seeking the help of a skilled practitioner or joining our group calls to receive help in this area. I have also included prayers at the end of this chapter to help release these things.

FALSE NEGATIVE CONTRACTS

I get so many clients who have been told that they have contracts to go through negative experiences in life: to get sick, to suffer, to be bonded with certain negative people. The whole idea of having an unbreakable contract from God that causes you to have and bear negative experiences is absolutely false. There are no such things as spiritual negative contracts that would cause people to suffer. But you can be influenced by negative ideas from others, by entities or mind control into believing this. This one idea causes people to not take responsibility for healing different aspects of their lives.

God wants us all to be happy and would never create such a thing as a negative contract binding people to suffer in order to work things through in their lives.

RADIONICS, CERN MACHINES, HAARP, AI AND MIND CONTROL

There are billions of radionics machines that are being used to target and destabilize humanity at this moment. They are being used both on the Earth and off planet to target and cut down the frequencies that humanity uses to manifest and create from. In the same respect, there are also cern machines, arrays of HAARP, AI and mind control machines which are also being used to harm and control people. All of these ultimately have the same purpose, to use frequency to undermine and scatter the vibrations and positive cycles within the human body in order to keep people easily distracted, easily controlled and emotionally imbalanced.

These electronic machines also tamper with a person's memory and emotions so people don't actually put the time in to do the manifesting work. They suddenly don't feel up to it or they actually forget to do it and can't make the consistent positive strides that are needed to create a lifestyle change.

Radionics machines can counteract any manifestation work that one may be doing. This is because the frequencies which would normally go out and assist in creating your dreams have been targeted, manipulated and destroyed by these machines. Without knowing about these interferences, one may assume that nothing is coming from their energetic or spiritual efforts to manifest when this is not true. It's just that a crucial aspect of what goes into energetically manifesting those dreams has been purposefully tampered with and eliminated.

TOXIC ENVIRONMENTS, LIFESTYLES AND RELATIONSHIPS

We live in an extremely toxic environment today and we are creating more pollution and toxins daily. We are collectively participating in this planetary problem and we are each individually deeply affected by it. Our foods, our water supplies, our lifestyles and our relationships bear so much of a toxic imprint that some may not even know what "healthy" actually looks like. Through stepping into divine alignment we can learn how to detoxify our relationships, our lifestyles and our environments. We can learn how to rebalance and restructure our world.

We can choose not to create more problems and we can avoid many of today's toxins through greater awareness and exercising our choices.

The more balanced our lifestyles and our bodies are, the more focused power we have to use in creating our dreams and goals. We are always in control of our choices. We must know and believe this. The more we strive for divine alignment the less toxic our lives become.

ANCESTRAL / GENETIC INFLUENCES

Some of the patterns that we came into this life to heal/rebalance in respect to our families can require a lot of our attention. They can be considered familial, systemic problems and can range from physical/genetic problems to habitual patterns and ancestral patterning. These are genetic and behavioral/mental/emotional patterns that have their beginnings long before your birth. All the same they are passed down to you through genetics and imprinting. They may demand some serious intervention on your part so as not to repeat the patterns of your ancestors should they differ from your highest and best.

Many spiritual traditions have an understanding that the starseeds, which also includes the indigo and crystal children, have been born into different families in order to heal the problems and patterns found in the world. In this way, through healing the family pieces, the family lineage is cleared of the negativity that is found in nearly all families on the planet today. When the family is cleared a piece of the planetary collective is cleared.

Respectfully, transmuting and healing family/genetic patterns can be a huge task. It is extremely important to have compassion and kindness towards yourself and all of those involved while doing this healing.

You can receive the help of a skilled practitioner or join one of our group calls to receive help. The "21 Heart Chakra Release" and "Whole Body Detox" meditations found on our meditation app are also extremely helpful when done on a daily basis. Receiving support in this process will greatly assist you in healing these patterns within yourself, within your lineage and within your life.

PAST LIFE / MULTIDIMENSIONAL INFLUENCES

Sometimes there can be aspects of other timelines, other life times or other dimensions that bleed into this one. In a general way, I call this esoteric transference. Sometimes we may have issues that we have not fully resolved in other life times / timelines. And while there is not a direct karmic transference, what can transfer is information that has leaked through or that you may need to continue to process while on your spiritual journey. The information may have to do with certain situations or people. Through using your intuition, you will understand how and why it's important.

The experience of esoteric transference may or may not be pleasant. If there is something here for you to see and understand, it is important for you to process the information or experiences in the most effective way you can. Doing this allows these experiences to resolve and integrate.

There are prayers in the back of the book to help with esoteric transference.

NEGATIVE MEDIA

There is so much media in the world today and people's minds are consumed by it from the moment they wake up often times to the moment they go to sleep. By far one of the most prevalent forms of negativity comes through the media. Media is extremely influential in shaping beliefs and ideas. Use judgement when choosing the TV shows, magazines, social media, books and music you consume. Everything you come into contact with is going to create an impact on your psyche and your vibration. Make your choices wisely.

GAMING / VIDEO GAMES

Online gaming and video games are creating a massive negative impact. They are destroying the capacity to focus. Focus is an important key in creating positive changes. In addition, gaming is skewing our imagination and sense of humanity. In the case of negative or violent games, they are dulling our sensitivity to violence and negative input, molding our perception, lowering our frequency, introducing more violence into our lives and conditioning us to make violent choices.

****

<u>THE LIGHT OF DIVINITY CAN SHINE INTO ANY NEGATIVITY IN MY LIFE AND CREATE POSITIVE OUTCOMES. GOD CAN HEAL ANY AND ALL SITUATIONS.</u>

****

Exercise #14

In your journal, write down all of the current negative experiences in your life, if any. List the possible sources and solutions. On a daily basis make an effort to reduce the negativity and create more healing in its place. Become fully committed to eliminating as much negativity as possible. Many times people have no concept of the fact that they can live free of negativity. If you apply yourself and approach clearing the negativity from your life with dedication and unconditional love you will have amazing results.

You will gain important insights, strength and resilience as you work through this.

HEALING PRAYERS / MAPS OF INTENT ESPECIALLY DESIGNED TO CLEAR AND PROTECT

All of the prayers below can be found in the back of this book. They can also be found on our prayer app. On the app you will hear my voice saying the prayers which lends powerful energetic support. You can schedule them to automatically play during the day in order to provide consistent assistance. Awareness, determination and consistency pay off when clearing negativity from your life.

PRAYER TO REMOVE AN ENTITY FROM A PERSON'S BODY

*This prayer must be said with absolute power, conviction and authority for the prayer to activate.

I am of God.
I ground myself to the Earth.

I command the Melchizedek Beings to open a portal from the Ultimate Dimension around (the person this prayer is for) and close it off underneath them.

I command the Melchizedek Beings to escort all of the negative entities and fractals thereof out of their body now.

I bless and forgive them for their manipulation and release them to the Ultimate Dimension with unconditional love and forgiveness.

I command that they place 12 Esoteric Merkaba Fields around the person this prayer is for with their sacral point in the center of the Merkaba Fields to protect them from any negative entities, fractals thereof, manipulations and transmissional frequencies that are not for their highest good through all space/time continuum in every dimension.

I thank you God and send you my unconditional love.
So Be It / Amen

PRAYER TO REMOVE MANIPULATION FROM YOUR PERSONAL LIFE

I am of God.

I ground myself to the Earth.

I command you, Dear God, to break all spells, curses, black magic and ancient rituals in my life that are not good and true.

I command you God to remove all negative remote viewers. Remove all radionics machines affecting my life now.

I command that you rebalance any manipulation of the space/time continuum in this 3rd Dimensional world and through all space/time continuum in every dimension.

I bring all the people involved with any of my personal manipulation infinite levels wide, infinite levels high, through all space/time continuum in every dimension before you God for justice in only the way you know how.

It is not for me to judge them, therefore I release them to you with unconditional love and forgiveness.

I thank you God and send you my unconditional love.
So Be It / Amen

PRAYER TO REMOVE SPIRITUAL ATTACKS

I am of God.

I ground myself to the Earth.

I command you Dear God to remove all the negative remote viewers, remove all manipulations and transmissional frequencies that are not for my highest good, through all space/time continuum in every direction.

Remove all machines and redundancies creating all these frequencies, infinite levels high, infinite levels wide, through all space/time continuum in every dimension no matter how remote.

I bring all of the beings involved with this before you God for justice in only the way you know how.

I release them to you God with unconditional love and forgiveness.

I thank you God and I send you my unconditional love.

So Be It / Amen

****
Any and all negativity can be healed with divine assistance and through stepping into divine alignment.

CHAPTER 15
FEAR, ANXIETY, ANGER, DEPRESSION AND STRESS

Today's fast paced and extremely stressful world can often give rise to numerous emotional and mental states that can perpetuate imbalance and disharmony. All of this can dramatically interfere with the capacity to manifest and maintain divine alignment. Fear, anxiety, anger, depression and stress are among the most prevalent negative emotions I see with my clients. For the most part, I suggest energy work to heal and release them.

As you step further into alignment, if you have any of these emotions trapped inside, they are going to be pushed to the surface. When this happens it's important to feel them, process them and release them. Depending on how long you have been experiencing these emotions they may have played a major role in your life. When you are ready to release them, make the decision to let them go once and for all. It's that simple. That's the first step. You may actually feel lonely or at a loss without these emotions and the problems and trauma that they've caused….and that you may have grown used to. Work through the loss also. This takes practice and vigilance. Vigilance is a strong word but it's fitting. We must stay on top of the different emotions we are offering out to the universe so that we can maintain the highest frequency and vibration at all times, especially when working through negativity.

In addition, you can receive additional energetic support when healing these emotions from a skilled energetic practitioner or by joining one of our online groups. You may also find using the meditations and prayers on our meditation and prayer apps helpful.

FEAR

Fear has been instilled in the majority of people from birth. In fact, most people find it more normal to experience some form of fear rather than experience some form of happiness and peace. Fear and violence in society and in the media barrage billions of people on the planet daily. Most recognize it but don't take the steps to move through and release it from their lives. They just live with it. Once you begin to intentionally move into divine alignment fear will come up to be dealt with if it is a part of your experience.

Releasing fear from your life is truly empowering. We can face the things that are making us afraid in addition to addressing the sources of fear. Remember to stay in the present moment, keep your frequency high and find things to be grateful for. Keep the channels open to your soul/higher self so that you can receive any divine energy and information you may need to help you transform the fears as they come up.

ANXIETY

Anxiety has recently moved from being an emotion that was caused primarily by overwhelm and exhaustion to one that is a chromic, sustained response, no matter what is going on. People these days are living in a continual state of anxiety even when things are going well. They can't seem to shake the feelings of anxiety, overwhelm and panic and move through them on their own. It becomes an experience that they may need help to remedy. Creating a calm and soothing environment, looking at all of the good that is happening and meditation are useful tools in healing anxiety. Consistency is important. Try different methods and when you find things that work continue to use them in order to create a routine that will help you heal and eliminate the anxiety.

ANGER

Anger is also another emotion that has become a chronic issue for many. In the past we became angry for a reason. Something adverse happened and we felt angry about it. Typically, one would have expressed themselves, had a conversation and released the emotion. Today however, with things becoming increasingly dysfunctional in the world, anger is a sustained emotion that people carry around with them some times for their whole lives. They ruminate and churn the anger inside of them. They are quick to flare and they have difficulty shaking it. In general, they have difficulty sustaining positive relationships and they may even need anger management classes.

Perhaps this was a behavior modelled in childhood. Perhaps they didn't have appropriate support to help them understand and work through their anger at critical points in their lives. Practicing present moment awareness, doing the "24 Heart Chakra Release" meditation daily and looking for things to be constantly grateful for, help transmute anger and allow it to dissipate.

DEPRESSION

Depression is an extremely common emotion today. Many times it's caused by the situations we face in life and many times it's also caused by the proliferation of toxins...including elfs, emfs, radionics, air pollution, noise pollution and negativity. We are increasingly cut off from each other. The TV and internet are our companions and our babysitters for our children. We are without the more traditional forms of support found in family and community. We are losing the understanding of social skills and how to appropriately relate to one another. We need one another. We were created to be together. Being cut off and feeling alone creates a sense of depression that could literally last a lifetime. Some people are on medication for depression for much of their lives and yet the symptoms may never cease. Seeking out skilled energy healers and doing inner work, practicing unity consciousness and gratitude go a long way in healing depression.

STRESS

Nearly everyone no matter what age or background is experiencing stress on a regular basis in today's world. It's almost as if our societal structures are creating stress for all of us. It's so common these days that I find that most people in the world are stressed. Even our animal companions are experiencing heightened and prolonged stress. It's everywhere. Prolonged exposure to any of the emotions in this chapter is not good but continuous chronic stress is extremely dangerous because stress kills. It causes the breakdown of the body system and it causes the symptomatology of disease to set in and replicate within the body. Today stress is the number one cause of many chronic and deadly diseases. We can take steps to free ourselves from stress and cultivate a relaxed, confident demeanor and mindset.

We can commit ourselves to creating the most loving attitude possible.

****

<u>I AM A DIVINE BEING. ALL STRESSFUL / NEGATIVE EMOTIONS CAN BE HEALED THROUGH EXPOSING THEM TO THE ENERGY AND UNCONDITIONAL LOVE OF GOD.</u>

****

<u>Exercise #15</u>

Pull out your journal. Write down some of the predominant negative emotions you are experiencing in your life, if any.

Next to each emotion write down the causes for it.

Write down how long each emotion has been present with you and whether or not you would consider it to be a triggered emotion or a chronic, long term state you are experiencing.

You can even go as far as writing down any "pay offs" that you are aware of that come from sustaining this emotion in your life. In other words, what are you getting out of behaving this way?

Monitor your emotions with present moment awareness. This allows any negative emotions to diffuse and shift. With consistent work you will be able learn how to stay in the present moment and respond instead of react.

Using meditation and energy work can prove invaluable in making steady and lasting progress.

****

God can balance and heal all negative emotions and difficult situations in our lives, allowing us to receive the gifts and the wisdom.

CHAPTER 16
CHANGE YOURSELF, CHANGE YOUR WORLD

I was sitting in Starbucks with only enough money in my pocket to buy coffee. Thank God for the free refills. I looked around at the people there and I realized that no one looked particularly happy and neither did I.

I had a huge "ah-ha" moment. Everyone in there seemed stuck in their negative emotions. I realized then and there that I could not afford to be in the same boat with them. In that moment I realized that I needed to change how I was looking at life. I realized that I had to actively embrace positivity if things were going to shift in my life.

I saw very clearly that in order to change your world or anything in your world, you must first change yourself.

I wanted to change everything about my life and I wanted to succeed again. I began to use positivity and gratitude in every aspect of my life. I noticed a difference immediately in how I felt...so much lighter and energetic. I had to accept these new feelings and the changes positivity brought without resistance. Slowly but surely everything in my life changed and moved forward.

Many of the current trends in the "manifesting movement" have focused on only using certain key principles like gratitude, forgiveness or the law of attraction. These are all extremely important. Over time an inner change can and will happen through using them. But if we understand that we have to change ourselves first in order for the outer to change, then we can create change faster. We don't move forward using different techniques and yet continue to be easily angered or consistently distracted by social media when it's inappropriate.

In the most complete sense, manifesting through divine alignment is a journey of transformation, evolution and growth.

It's all about who we are "being" right now and who we are becoming.

What do we have to think, feel, believe and do in order to access alignment right now? Who do we have to become in order to live the divine plan of our lives?

I had to change nearly everything in my life in order to become who I am today.

I had to shift my intentions and thoughts. I was always principled but when I surrendered my life to God, I had to allow God to create my life and show me who I was meant to be.

Surrendering how the money came in was just the first step. I had to become aware of how the healings were to proceed, what God wanted from me, and how God wanted to move the ministry forward. I had to change the way I was used to experiencing life and I had to process a lot of emotion and past experiences in order to become clearer and more whole.

God initiated and created these changes within me. I surrendered and followed through. I didn't have to change a few things and then suddenly everything was set. I had to change nearly every aspect of my life.

I have to face change on a daily basis.
Change is actually the constant.

Think about the life you would like to manifest. Think about the different circumstances and opportunities you would like to experience. When you picture the things you want to manifest are there any things that you realize you need to change about yourself in order to create the version of you that can co-create, accept and experience your dreams?

Whatever changes need to be made in your life, begin to make them now. There are so many different ways that change may be waiting to happen.

Who do you have to become in order to bring your gifts in fully? Do you have to learn any new skills or practice any processes? Who do you have to be in order to create a truly satisfying, happy life and allow yourself to experience and receive abundance on all levels?

As we change our world changes.

When we become the person who is in alignment and who can activate the potentials we want to experience in our lives, our manifestations accelerate.

No matter where you are in your life, no matter what age or the circumstance, you can change to become the person who can live out your dreams and move your dreams forward.

Daily, consistent changes create lasting alignment. It explains how I went from being financially bankrupt to being a successful healer with a thriving business. So much in my life has changed. I embrace the changes. I am creating more, serving more, experiencing more abundance and enjoying myself more now than ever before.

Whatever changes you feel you need to make, make them. Feel confident about yourself. Don't be afraid. Realize that God is with you through all of these changes. You are not doing this alone.

As you align with the changes God is seeking to make in your life...as you ask more of yourself and hold yourself accountable for maintaining divine alignment, your world and your life will shift to reflect the divine plan flowering within your life.

Daily, consistent changes add up.

****

<u>**CHANGE IS CONSTANT.**</u>
<u>**AS I CHANGE MYSELF, MY WORLD CHANGES. I LOVE AND EMBRACE WHO I AM AND WHO I AM BECOMING.**</u>

****

Exercise #16

Pull out your journal.

Make a list of things that you could change within yourself (perhaps how you are thinking or behaving) that could create more positive results. What changes could you make in your life that will help you achieve greater alignment?

Could you become more compassionate or is there something you could do like clear out a closet and give things away?

Find one thing that you could do today that will create a change in the right direction and take the time to do it.

As you go through the process, add more things to the list of what you could change until you feel like you are living in greater alignment.

Stay committed to changing one thing a week. The vibrancy, joy and success in your life will increase.

As you follow your inner guidance in creating these changes, the Divine will assist you in manifesting your fullest joy and potential.

*Take it up a level…

Make a list of all of the things that are creating problems, drama or setbacks in your life.

Be very honest.

Don't make excuses about how and why the problem exists. If you feel led to include it, include it.

Are you drinking or smoking in an imbalanced way? Are you experiencing abusive relationships? Are you involved with people who are draining or overly needy? Regardless of the "whys", these kinds of relationships are difficult and create imbalances.

Do you have any addiction issues? This can be internet or social media addictions also not only substances or behaviors.

Are you rude and/or impatient at times? Are you distracted by friends or on the smart phone/internet when your children are talking to you?

Take account of where and how the negativity is coming into your life. Make a list and make a plan to honestly change it with kindness and compassion towards yourself. Who you are and who you are becoming rests on your character. Allow yourself to be the best you possible. Love the person in the mirror. Allow them to soar through the changes you embrace.

****

*EMBRACE THE CHANGES THAT ARE WAITING. LIFE IS GLORIOUS. YOU CAN HAVE ALL THAT GOD HAS MADE READY FOR YOU AND ALL OF THE BEAUTIFUL DREAMS OF YOUR HEART. MAKE THE CHANGES IN YOUR LIFE AND WATCH WHAT HAPPENS.

CHAPTER 17
EMBRACING YOUR IMAGINATION / CREATING A LIST

There is an old saying, that God gives us the desires of our heart and the capacity to manifest them. This is true.

Unfortunately, many people have not given themselves permission to have what they really want usually because they don't believe they can have it. Instead, they pursue things they don't truly want only because they believe that it's the best they can do. Eventually they manifest the experiences they believe they can have.

It's important to feel deserving in order to receive. Otherwise, we end up resisting or repelling the things we want.

If we could look at life through a fresh perspective, without denying ourselves the things that bring us joy, life would be very different. We would find that we could create our dreams easily. We would have no problems in allowing and embracing happiness.

If you haven't done so already, create a manifesting list. Write down the things you would like to experience in your life. These should be things and experiences that will bring you joy and happiness. Get as specific as possible and let your heart soar as you describe all of the things that you are working towards achieving.

Some people make a special activity out of it. They use beautiful paper, write out their list consciously and even put stickers, glitter or pictures on it.

Do whatever inspires you. When you are done, add this statement to the beginning of your list…

"In ease and grace and in the highest and best for all, I choose to manifest…"

Add this at the end, after the list.

"All this or better I am lovingly open to receive and have in order to create the highest good in my life. I am so grateful to you God. Thank you so much."

If it feels right for you, place the list where you can see it on a daily basis. Some people place it near their bedside so that they can see it first thing in the morning and last thing at night. Some people place it close to the bathroom mirror so they see it every time they go into the washroom. Some people place their list in their wallet or purse so that they can look at it during the day.

When you look at your list go deeply into gratitude. Try to feel the way you would if you already had these things. Really bring up the most powerful emotions you can in order to step into the frequency of the things on your list.

Doing this creates an energetic connection between you and your goals. It helps them to manifest faster.

One of the biggest things that endows us to create is the ability to imagine. Einstein once said: "The capacity to imagine is more important than knowledge. For knowledge is limited whereas imagination embraces the entire world, stimulating progress, giving birth to evolution." When we can develop our imagination and use it constructively, we reach our goals faster. The imagination sends messages to the subconscious and the inner divine. In each case something different happens. The imagination sends a message to the subconscious, repatterning it, allowing it to be more magnetic and open to the things that you're seeking to create. The imagination also informs God, the soul and your inner self as to what you're working towards.

In response, the Divine will send messages through a person's intuition as to how to proceed in moving closer to attaining one's goals. Use your imagination intentionally. Increase your vibration through allowing yourself to imagine better and better outcomes and situations. Let your imagination help you bolster your creative process.

Your imagination is an aspect of your divine power that exists to help you manifest into the physical. Use it wisely.

When working to manifest a relationship remember that you cannot manifest a particular person to love you but you can imagine the kind of relationship you would like to have. List the different qualities that you would like in a mate and in the relationship. Doing this will allow God to bring you the right person at the right time. In the meantime, look at yourself and prepare yourself to be in a great relationship. Ask yourself some honest questions. Are you committed to being a good partner? Are you compassionate and kind? Are you a good listener? How is your self-esteem? Would you be able to receive a wonderful partner if one came to you or would you feel undeserving and then unconsciously self-sabotage? Whatever needs to be addressed in a holistic way to get you prepared for your positive relationship, do that now.

Look at the other things on your list and do the same to the best of your ability. If moving to a new home is on your list, imagine all of the things you would love to have in your home. Imagine yourself already living there. Imagine all of your happiness waking up and having breakfast there.

Begin to give or throw away things that you may no longer need or enjoy. Make space so that you can move forward faster. When the possibilities begin to show themselves you will be able to make the move in an easier way because you have been preparing for it. If making a career change is on your list, research and prepare yourself to move into your new career.

As you go over your list daily remember that it's important to believe that all of the things that you are seeking to manifest already exist. They are not far off in the distance somewhere. Experience them being here in the now as you are imagining them.

All of the possibilities of what you are seeking to experience exist right now.

You may not be experiencing them in this moment but they are already here. You just have to raise your frequency to match the frequency of the experience. Keep your frequency high and take inspired action.

After you have made your list, fill it with love and gratitude. Sending love and appreciation to your list will help to create a stronger conduit to draw these situations and things into your life faster.

Your list holds the energy of your dreams and your contribution to the world. Rejoice in it. Feel it. Allow it. Align with it. Love it. Celebrate it.

Imagine your life as you would like it to be.
Dream deeply.
Feel it as though you were already experiencing it.

****
THE DIVINE HAS A WONDERFUL LIFE PLANNED FOR ME. I AM OPEN TO RECEIVING IT NOW. THROUGH FOLLOWING MY JOY, I ALLOW MYSELF TO HAVE AND EXPERIENCE GOD'S GIFTS FOR ME.
****

Exercise #17

At least once a day connect with your higher self/inner guidance and ask specifically to be guided to the next right action to take in order to manifest your dreams.

Every time you look at your list go into love and gratitude and then release it to the Divine. Get very clear visions about what you are seeking to manifest and then let it go. Doing this will allow you to focus on your guidance and intuition. When you get the guidance or information from the Divine be sure to act on it as quickly as possible. Getting authentic guidance to do something and then taking action on it opens the floodgates to more opportunities. Inversely, getting guidance and not taking action on it usually stalls information from coming to you in the future and slows the whole process of manifesting down.

Stay focused on all the good already in your life and how your dreams are manifesting. This will keep your frequency up and usher in your dreams faster.

Exercise #17b

Get specific. Create a visual picture in your mind of what you are seeking to co-create with the Divine. If you know you want a four-bedroom home for you and your family to live in safely and comfortably, make sure you list some of the details and specifics you would like in your home. If you are looking to attract a soul mate and life partner, write down some of the specific experiences you would love to have.

If you are looking to create more vibrancy in your health or if you are seeking a career change, get very specific with certain experiences and qualities you would like to have. In as much detail as possible describe what you feel you are seeking to attract and experience. This will help you gain greater clarity about what brings you joy and what you are moving towards.

****
Energy flows where intention and attention goes.

CHAPTER 18
MONEY AND FINANCIAL ABUNDANCE

The world that we live in today is largely dependent on money. We use it on a continual, daily basis to acquire nearly everything we have and use.

And yet so many people have issues and problems with it.

They believe certain things about it. They feel certain things towards it. They base their self-worth on how much of it they have or don't have. They judge and scrutinize others based on how much of it they have and how they use it. The media focuses in on and glorifies those who have it. It takes up a lot of bandwidth in our culture.

People are triggered by what they experience around it. One of the biggest causes of failed marriages is money. Not the relationship itself. Money.

It's obvious that as a collective we need to reframe what we experience and believe about it.

Our skewed beliefs around it cause us to create competition, stress and sickness. Many people spend a large hunk of their lives worrying about it. This worry causes constriction and ages people.

Sometimes we feel guilty about money if we have it and others don't. We might feel compromised when we have it in the face of so much suffering in the world.

We might also have negative beliefs about it, ie., "People who have it are mean and unscrupulous."

In creating alignment it's important to be in balance in all areas of our lives…including around money and financial abundance.

We can change our beliefs around money at any moment to beliefs that serve us all.

We all could do so much good out in the world if we all had more than enough money. Through becoming prosperous and having a loving response to money we can decrease our stress and the stress in the world. We can care for ourselves and our families better when we imagine and create a prosperous world.

What if everyone had more than enough money without money losing its value? What if all of the problems that are created by poverty and "lack of" were nonexistent because everyone was prosperous, successful, happy and fulfilled? The planet would rise in vibration and the environment would be cared for and healed. And while money doesn't make people happy or fulfilled it can help decrease stress and suffering. It buys us the things that we want, use and need. It's important to find a way to get it into the hands of all of the people who want to do good things with it.

We need to find a way to respect and honor money while respecting and honoring ourselves when we have it. People sometimes get egotistical, vain, lustful and greedy when they have it. They get a false sense of self, feel superior to others or entitled when they have it. Many times these behaviors make others not want to have it.

The truth is that money is just energy. It's neutral. We decide how we use it. We decide what we feel about it. We decide how it affects us.

Regardless of any of our fears or beliefs around money, financial abundance is everyone's birthright.

Money allows people to have greater freedom. It allows people to give generously. It allows us to help others and eliminate stress from their lives. It allows us to pick and choose what we want to experience.

Let us use it in service to share our gifts and heal the world. Imagine a world free of money stress. Take a deep breath on that.

If everyone in the world today was suddenly free of financial problems and debt, the entire planet would be a different place.

You can visualize this or better for everyone in the world. Because the truth is the world we live in is wildly abundant.

Nature is over the top abundant. The seashore has billions of grains of sand. The oceans are vast and unlimited. The stars in the sky are unlimited and shine from horizon to horizon It is within our inner programming to be over the top abundant. Our negative beliefs and our hang ups around money create what we experience around money.

Let us remember to allow money in and to use our money in service to the world. In addition, let us use the power of our intention and visualization to visualize a world without money problems, a world where everyone has more than enough and is abundantly provided for. This is the divine plan.

****

<u>MONEY IS EVERYWHERE. THERE IS NO LACK OF IT. I AM WILLING TO LET IT IN. I AM WILLING TO ALLOW IT TO SERVE ME AND HELP ME.</u>

****

<u>Exercise #18</u>

This is a visualization exercise.

Take some quiet time when you will not be disturbed. Imagine that you are on a beautiful golden bridge of light. Imagine that you are planning to have a conversation with money on this bridge. When money shows up, it can be in any form that feels right to you. You can see money as a person or a thing. Allow money to look or have the appearance of any idea that you choose.

When money comes, talk to it about the different things that have been happening in your life because of it or because of the lack of it. Have an honest conversation about all that is happening and all that you would like to see happening in the future.

Have the intention to become friends with money. You may not feel ready to do this in this conversation but perhaps you can commit to revisiting money on the golden bridge and furthering your relationship with it at a later time. This one intention to become friends with money will create change and positive movement.

Be willing to be loving towards money. It's hard to attract something or be close with someone if deep down inside you have conflicting beliefs around them that are actually pushing them away. Money is no different.

Exercise #18b

Pull out your journal, come up with five projects or ways that you intend to use money to benefit yourself and others when you have more of it.

Dream big and over the top for this one. Maybe you would start a children's school that would help at risk youth understand their innate beauty and divinity. Maybe your school would focus in on social skills, community, self-love, self-empowerment and creativity.

Maybe you would fund a project to clean up all of the trash in the oceans. Imagine you have so much money that you can do this. Maybe you have a dream to help single mothers and their children...giving them housing and sending their kids to school, kindergarten through college. Maybe you will build energy efficient, solar powered, green homes and schools and create a co-op to teach others how to do the same.

Spend some time with this and recognize that your energy and financial input can and will change the world. Through healing and embracing any issues you may have with money you will create balance in the world and you will be an example and inspiration to others to do the same.

Exercise #18c

Reverse the flow and see money coming to you. Those who do this report an increase of money and abundance coming to them. You can call money to you through using different affirmations that make a positive difference to you.

Affirmations like:
"Money comes to me easily and effortlessly."

"I deserve abundance, peace and financial freedom. I am willing to allow it in and receive it."

"I love how money helps me. I love what it does for the world."

"Wealth serves me. I love using it to achieve beautiful goals."

See and feel money coming freely to you from every direction in this exercise. Practice this exercise for at least 5 minutes at a time.

****
ALLOW MONEY TO BE YOUR FRIEND. ALLOW IT TO HELP AND SERVE YOU.

CHAPTER 19
INTENTION

The gift of intention is like the steering system of your creative process. In using the gift of intention, we create a link to the things we want to manifest and bring them into our world through the magnetic pull of our focused energy. We are made to have the divine desires of our heart. In holding our intention strong on a daily basis we step closer to our dreams and our dreams move closer to us. In short, your intentions will help you take greater control of your life.

A working definition of intention is: "To have in mind a purpose or a plan, to direct the mind, to aim."

Lacking intention, we sometimes stray without meaning or direction. But with it, all the forces of the universe can align to make even the impossible, possible. Always remember… "What you create in your mind, you create in your reality."

You do this through holding your intention.

Manifesting a dream begins by setting an intention.

Intention is coming into balanced acceptance.
Intention is holding clear vision.
Intention is setting your mind to it, deciding "this or better", and allowing it to happen.

Intention is power. Get clear and use it. Firmly intend that you are going to allow the divine plan of your life to unfold. Intend that you are going to do whatever you are led to do and take whatever steps your guidance prompts you to take when the information comes to you. Not only do we hold the intention for the things on our list…we intend to follow through and do whatever our inner prompting suggests in order to move forward.

Remember that energy flows where intention goes. Hold your attention on your list while holding your intention to create it. If your intent is clear, it will move your manifesting along faster.

Firmly intend to manifest your dreams and then demand more of yourself. If/when situations arise where you feel resistance to following through, process any doubts, fears, problems or self-sabotage patterns that you notice. Should this happen, set your intention to double your effort and then take action. Set your intention every new day and as you go through the day.

When you awake, set your intention to have a great day. When you do your spiritual/energy work, set your intention to make the most of it and to make progress. When you are driving around town, intend to have a safe drive. When you are creating, intend to remain inspired and open to creating the best. When you prepare to rest, intend to rest well. When you pray, intend to bring the most you can to it. When you cook, intend to create something wonderful and delicious.

When you set your intention, intend to stay in joy and gratitude as much as possible. The emotions within you magnetize your dreams to you. Intend to experience the emotions that you will feel when your dreams come to you. Hold your intention strong every day, take guided steps to bring it into fruition, then completely surrender it to God. Let it all go. You will feel a calm certainty and you will know that the energy will return to you in the most positive way at the right time.

Setting your intention daily will help you stay focused. It will fuel the process of change that you have to go through in order to manifest your dreams and it will help and support you in maintaining divine alignment and living the divine plan.

****

<u>MY INTENTION IS CRYSTAL CLEAR.</u>
<u>I INTEND TO CREATE AND LIVE THE</u>
<u>DIVINE PLAN OF MY LIFE.</u>

****

<u>Exercise #19</u>

Look over your manifesting list and gauge what your level of intention is with each thing. On a scale from 1-10 gauge how strong your intention is for each thing? Some things may be easier to have a strong intention for. Spend some time gaining clarity about any resistance or stuck feelings you may have. Does the work until you feel clear and your intention is strong for each thing? The clearer your intention, the stronger it is and the more it can do for you. The clearer it is the more powerfully it can and will draw to you what you are seeking to create.

Do some journaling about how strong your intention feels every day, how things are happening in your life and how you are responding to it. Throwing a heavy dose of gratitude in for the power of your intention will help you to grow stronger and more appreciative of how your intention is shaping your world.

Exercise #19b

On a daily basis, sometime soon after waking, set your intention to succeed. Get clear and strong about your intention to create greater flow and success in your life.

Remember to always see yourself as a success…whether it's a success in maintaining alignment, accessing the divine plan or creating your life through using your gifts. Whatever the case see yourself as being successful.

***████

Intend to create beauty, goodness and greatness. Intend to allow yourself to receive and experience alignment. Intend to step into the divine pan of your life.*

CHAPTER 20
INTUITION AND INSPIRED ACTION

Our intuition is given to us by God, our soul/higher self and the Divine. It provides us with the exact information we need to make choices and take specific actions. When we use our intuition, we take advantage of God's gifts. Through following our intuition, we access divine alignment and we take inspired action.

When we get information through our intuition, it's important to act on it as soon as possible. Waiting to act on it or hesitating can allow fear or subconscious patterns to step in. When the universe sends messages it's watching our response to see how serious we are about making change and about staying in alignment. Sometimes you may feel like you are being tested by the Divine. It may be better to look at it like the universe is challenging you to expand past your limits and grow. As you take inspired action and begin to see all that you are capable of, your outlook and belief systems will change to reflect your increasing happiness and new successes. Consistently following your intuitive leads and taking inspired action will eventually lead to harmony and balance in all areas of your life.

When we get into the habit of taking inspired action we build a muscle around consistently following our guidance. This changes us and dissolves our subconscious beliefs. Our belief in our self grows. We become increasingly confident that we can do new and different things. We realize that we can move into new arenas successfully and that we are capable of things we may have not realized were possible before.

When we embrace our intuition we allow divine wisdom to guide us. It challenges us and we evolve into better versions of ourselves.

I use my intuition constantly throughout the day. It's a crucial aspect of my work. I have to receive accurate information about what God wants me to do in my sessions. Through using it, I am able to help people heal and transform. I am able to be of service to the world.

Some people would say that intuition is a hunch. I would expand that definition. It is always based on receiving information specifically related to how to proceed. It can be as subtle as a hunch and it can be as specific and as powerful as a direct message to your consciousness.

Intuition is accurate all of the time. This is why it's so important to make sure that your intuition has been clarified and that you are actually hearing your highest guidance as opposed anything else like your ego or negative subconscious patterns. Once you start to use your intuition these aspects of yourself may seek your attention and could work to derail you. This is because you are changing and moving out of your comfort zone. These parts of yourself are comfortable in the role they have had in running the show in your life. Once you begin to make your intuition your main source of guidance, you may face inner resistance as these other parts of yourself seek to do things that are not as threatening as moving forward may be.

It may take some time to truly clarify your intuition but once you do this and become solidly established in it, you will see how God is always focused on helping you have the best life possible.

When you are using your intuition you may feel body responses. You may feel a lightness when you are following through. You may feel a heaviness or dragginess when you are not listening.

If you are not used to listening to your inner guidance, work to change this. Intuition is the key to accessing divine alignment and the divine plan. There are online sites which offer exercises, ideas and courses to help you develop your intuition. Daily practice yields consistent results.

As you follow your intuition, the intuitive leads will increase. This also means that your inspired action will increase. You will find yourself constantly stepping out of your comfort zone and facing things that are new and exciting. These new experiences may also be scary and challenging at times.

Our intuition constantly guides us to take bigger steps up, to experience more joy and success, and to expand our horizons and well-being. Eventually you will create a new comfort zone, one that is defined by positive experiences, joy and alignment. Our intuition is our internal GPS.

Imagine that you have found yourself in an unfamiliar neighborhood and you choose not to use your GPS. You could spend a lot of time being lost and confused. You may be in an unsafe area. You may have some things you need to get done but you can't do them because you're lost. Most people would definitely use their GPS under such circumstances. In the same way it's important to always use our intuition in order to navigate successfully through life. It's always there for us. It's always working. It's always accurate.

If you don't follow it, however, it will decrease. This is because God isn't going to force you to accept divine help. The less you rely on it, the harder it will be to hear and distinguish. This is because by not listening, you have chosen not to use it. God honors your choices and pulls the intuition back. Inversely, should you choose to use it, you will notice that it will increase in strength and presence.

Some people may misinterpret the notion of consistently following your intuition with the loss of freedom. This is actually the opposite of what happens. Listening to your intuition increases your freedom and personal power. It helps you to stay safe, healthy and in the right places at the right times. It insures the highest outcomes in all cases. It creates win-win situations for all involved and works to bring about harmony and growth. It brings us into divine alignment and helps us live the divine plan. You will grow closer in your relationship with God.

Follow your intuition lovingly, fearlessly and courageously. You will find yourself walking in the midst of the Divine.

****

<u>GOD COMMUNICATES TO ME THROUGH MY INTUITION HELPING ME TO MAKE THE BEST CHOICES AT ALL TIMES. I FOLLOW MY INTUITION AND TAKE INSPIRED ACTION AS THE INFORMATION COMES TO ME.</u>

****

Exercise #20

Because you are reading this book, you are most likely familiar with and use your intuition, at least to some extent. Take some time to really evaluate how often you listen to your intuition. Do you listen constantly or only once in a while?

Notice what happens when you listen to it and what happens when you don't. Usually when we don't listen things don't go as well and sometimes things may even go awry. In any moment however you can get things back on track by listening and following through. It's important to realize that if you haven't been in the habit of listening 100% it could take a while to build up the muscle to consistently follow your intuition.

Make sure that you spend quiet meditative time daily to allow yourself to receive messages and information from the Divine. Work to open up and allow yourself to experience your intuition.

If you feel blocked in listening to your intuition you may want to visit the prayer for removing subconscious blocks in the back of the book. There may be a bigger issue around self-love, self-care or worthiness that you need to address. Once you get clear on your resistance, do the work to heal it and then reassert yourself.

This is an easy process to build up. Simply begin to actively listen to and follow your intuition constantly. Notice how your life changes for the better. Your intuition is always working to help you. Relax in the awareness that God is always with you...showering you with solutions and ideas to help you succeed in life.

Exercise #20b

Using journal entries write down what you are being guided to do and write down what happened after you took action. What do you feel about your guidance? Did you have any emotional response to it? If so, how did you handle your emotions? What were your expectations about taking action? What happened after you took action? How did your experience with God shift, grow or change?

Write about your daily actions in relation to your intuition. As you look back over your entries you will see the journey of your soul. Doing this daily will help you to feel supported. You will be able to track the journey of God activating the divine plan within your life. Journaling in this way will help to keep your resolve strong and your determination firm.

****

Follow your intuition unerringly. It will provide you with the most reliable information to help you navigate your life with joy and love. Following it brings happiness, abundance and peace.

CHAPTER 21
FOCUS-THE KEY

When we focus, we are using the spiritual power within us to create.

Focused attention works like a magnifying glass. It condenses your energy and amplifies the power of whatever ideas and frequencies you send out. It creates a tremendous magnetic pull that will move people, places and things towards you to help you to create your goals and dreams.

What you focus on receives your energy and begins to manifest in the same way that a tiny seed planted in the earth receives water and sunlight and then starts to grow.

What you focus on expands and as you notice the positive results of your focused energy, the power and rate of your manifestations increase.

Focus and notice what is going on around you. Focus and notice the changes that you are creating. Focus and respond positively.

The more you notice the results of your focused attention the better things will get. The noticing is as important as the focusing because it's like giving feedback to the universe that…" yes" this is what you want. It's like a 2 sided creative coin that is a super charged magnet pulling in more of what you want.

Stay focused on what you are creating and stay focused on all the good that is happening. Our beliefs determine how we use our focus. So in order to get the most out of our capacity to focus we may have to change the nature of what and how we believe.

As mentioned before, we make our choices based our beliefs but these beliefs may or may not be true. We have to look at how we are focused on our beliefs, on what is actually true and on what is possible.

You may believe that it's easy for other people to succeed but not you. This is a very common belief. Begin to look at all of the ways where you have already experienced success. Understand that since you succeeded before you can do it again. Focus on that. Believe that since others have done this that you can do it too. Believe that your success already exists. Focus on showing yourself this. Focus on noticing what is currently working right for you. Focus on remembering where things went right for you in the past so that you can use this as a reference point and build your confidence and self-esteem.

The art of focusing is really the art of constructive thinking. Most people are not used to controlling their thoughts. They let their thoughts run rampant. And because creation happens through what we focus on, it's important to be selective and careful about what we allow ourselves to think. We have to use our power of focus purposefully. What we take our time to think about manifests into what we are choosing to experience. It all goes together.

Look at where your thoughts usually drift to. What kind of things do you normally focus on? What kinds of things are you experiencing in your life? Can you see any correlation in how your focused thought is creating the experiences you are having? So many people are giving their thoughts to stressful situations or the internet or to online distractions like social media or gaming. Whatever you focus on vibrationally creates more of the same.

The universe expands and grows through our creative energy. This was originally intended to happen through the power of love. Thinking was originally intended to be closely linked to the art of receptivity, where we were receiving ideas from the Divine and then acting on them. The whole process was intended to be co-creative. This is not what most of the world is experiencing today.

Our minds have become so cluttered with random thoughts and with compulsive "busyness" that many of us are not intentionally using our minds to actively create what we want.

When we look at the world today we can see how these thoughts can work against us.

We have to have discipline and discernment around what we give our attention and time to. Otherwise, we may face a barrage of confusion and negativity from outside sources as our thoughts return to us in form. This is where strengthening our minds and the power of our resolve comes into play. We have to be careful in what we expose ourselves to and what we give our attention to.

We have to be consistent and diligent in this because it directly affects the quality of our lives.

If we are having problems focusing, we must face this and change it.

Unfortunately, most people today are losing IQ points. In fact, the IQ is falling rampantly, especially in America. This is primarily due to our modern lifestyle. We are losing the power to focus and in turn our capacity to manifest our dreams. When our minds are scattered, our power is scattered and our results are scattered.

Our thoughts are increasingly disorganized, anxious and stressed and so are our lives. Within the medical profession, the diagnosis for Attention Deficit Disorder or ADD is on a continual rise as more and more people are finding themselves in crippling situations because of their inability to focus and make positive change.

We need to be able to focus in order to move forward in our lives.

In order to regain our focus, as well as raise our IQs and the quality of our lives we can begin to incorporate some simple, holistic practices.

-Practice present moment awareness.

-Set your intention to unify with the divine mind/consciousness. This will help to expand your consciousness and raise the frequency of your thoughts.

-Spend more time in nature and allow it to nurture and inform you.

-Decrease your exposure to negative information and stressful situations.

-Stay in gratitude.

-Meditate. Meditation really helps with focus and it will help you maintain your connection to God.

The more focused we are on the good, the better we create, the more powerful we become.

When you focus on positivity, joy and beauty your outer world transforms. The stronger your focus, the easier it is for you to intentionally manifest.

Allowing ourselves to focus on goodness and all that we choose to experience will strengthen our resolve, surround us in beauty and usher in the divine plan of our lives.

****
<u>THE DIVINE PLAN OF MY LIFE UNFOLDS AS I FOCUS IN ON IT, NOTICE THE CHANGES AND CONTINUE TO TAKE ACTION.</u>
****

Exercise #21

Take out your journal. Write down any areas where you notice you have problems with focus. Do you notice this more in the morning or in the evening? Is this related to certain subjects or tasks?

Seek to eliminate different activities which create problems with focusing like extended internet use, negative environments and people, and difficult situations. Make sure that you are getting the needed amounts of rest daily. Realize that regaining a sense of focus is a practiced discipline that can be aided through daily meditation, proper nutrition and energy work.

If need be, you may want to consider receiving energy sessions from a skilled practitioner. You can also join one of our group calls.

Exercise #21b

Take 5-10 minutes every morning and meditate.

There are an assortment of meditation techniques online. Learn about them and experiment. Find one that you feel comfortable using on a daily basis.

The following is an all-purpose, simple form of meditation that's very effective.

Make sure that you have a half hour of undisturbed time.
Sit in a relaxed posture. Allow your mind to focus on your breathing. As your thoughts come, gently allow them to pass through without engaging or judging them. Simply continue to refocus yourself on your breathing.

As you focus on the breath you will notice more and more pauses in the thinking and you will be able to discernibly experience the places where you are in stillness, silence and peace.

****
Focus in and appreciate all of the goodness that is happening in your life right now. Notice all that you are capable of and all that the Divine is doing for you.

CHAPTER 22
DETERMINATION / COMMITMENT

New and unfamiliar experiences and challenges come up once a person decides to change. Without the solid commitment and determination, it takes to follow through, many fall by the wayside without ever reaping the benefits of what they've started.

Taking full responsibility for changing your life is crucial. Remembering your decision to access divine alignment and the divine plan on a daily basis will help support you through the changes inherent in his journey. Some of what may come up may not be easy to deal with. This is why it's important to stay committed and determined. This is part of what it is to grow into spiritual maturity.

Restoring divine alignment is an alchemical process. It isn't linear and the more changes you make in one area, be it physical, mental, emotional, etc., the more other areas are also affected. Things move around and shift and challenges appear that weren't there before because you are changing from an old paradigm into an entirely new and different lifestyle and reality.

Once I completely surrendered my life to God, my life began to change in unimaginable and unpredictable ways. I wasn't trying to control any of it. I held firm to my decision to let God take the lead in my life. In this I have been committed and determined and what has emerged has been spectacular.

When I was homeless, I knew that I was not experiencing all that God had for me. I knew that I was the one who had to face the things that were out of alignment. I took full responsibility for what had to change. No one else could do this for me.

I couldn't allow fear, conditioning, laziness, procrastination or any form of negativity to get in my way. I couldn't allow what anyone thought of me to distract me or weaken my resolve. Steadily and surely, everything changed for the better. And while I am facing totally different scenarios today, my commitment and determination to follow the divine plan of my life are stronger today than ever. Without firm resolve, I wouldn't have been able to accomplish what I have because there were many situations that were extremely difficult and challenging. Through it all, I held on to the fact that God supports me 100%. I moved forward taking whatever steps I was guided to take, holding firm to my decision and commitment. In this way, I arrived at the life that I am currently living now.

God only gave me situations and opportunities that I could actually handle. All of it was within my reach even though many times I've had to stretch.

From my experience, God doesn't give all the steps to create divine alignment in one huge hunk. Usually we get information about what we are to do in small doable pieces. God knows what we can master in a day, in a few days or over a period of time and this is what we are usually guided to work with.

I was also very clear about the fact that the divine plan for my life already existed. God created it long before I was ever born. All I had to do was access it. It took an incredible amount of perseverance and years of transforming my life to fully access it. But I never felt vague about what I was seeking to achieve. It was already mine and it already existed. I just needed to get fully into divine alignment, learn what I needed to know and make the necessary changes while moving forward.

I did all that I could to stay in alignment and to stay positive and focused. I felt compelled to change myself. I wanted to be the person God knew I could be. I thank my sense of commitment for helping me to stay strong through all of the different obstacles and challenges and for helping me step into the divine plan of my life.

Many people who have achieved success attribute it to sheer determination and resolve. Granted there is another important factor known as divine timing which is God's timing in all things. In addition, it may not turn out exactly the way you imagined or in the time frame you imagined but if you stay committed it will turn out brilliantly according to God's direction. Sometimes there is a lot more to go through and a lot more to work through than we could have possibly imagined in order to fully live the divine plan of our lives. This is why holding firm to your choice to access alignment and staying determined are so important.

We are stronger and more powerful than we are led to believe.

Make a commitment to yourself and to the divine plan of your life now. Take daily steps and notice the difference staying in a committed mindset makes. Hold fast to your determination and you will see your life unfold according to God's plan for you. You will feel the love and presence of God in your life in a way that you may not have before. And you will recognize yourself as a powerful divine being capable of manifesting unlimited goodness in your life.

****

<u>I AM DETERMINED AND COMMITTED TO LIVE MY LIFE THROUGH DIVINE ALIGNMENT AND TO MANIFEST GOD'S PLAN FOR MY LIFE.</u>

****

<u>Exercise #22</u>

Using your journal, go through your manifesting list. Rate how determined and committed you are to manifesting your goals. Be honest and get a feel in your body about your level of commitment.

Gauge how committed you have been thus far to creating the goals on your list. Rate your level of determination on a scale of 1-10 for each thing.

Doing this will allow you to see how you are feeling about your goals. This will give you needed insight to help you manifest better.

After you gauge your level of determination for each item on your list, look at the items that you are not 100% committed to creating. If necessary, remove them from your list until you are truly committed to doing what it takes to create them. You can always return to them later.

For everything on your list, monitor your commitment weekly. At the end of each week review your emotions and the actions you were guided to take to create change.

****
STAY COMMITTED. STAY DETERMINED.

CHAPTER 23
THE COMPANY WE CHOOSE /
NO HOLDING BACK

God works through people to help us create our lives. In turn, we create our lives through our relationships and through our communities. Opportunities and growth come to us through others. Money comes to us through others. Love and abundance comes to us through others. Our relationships allow us to expand our visions and our careers. Our purpose is expressed and moves out into the world through the help of other people. We in turn support and help others through the work we do and through sharing our gifts, our time, our energy and our love.

Initially, we may not be aware of the importance of the company we keep. We are born into families and into certain social groups. As we grow, we attract and surround ourselves with people who share the same views and ideas as we do. Typically, the people in our lives mirror our own qualities back to us, good, bad, creative, lazy, happy, controversial, reserved, inspired, etc. They mirror our ideas and any judgements we may have back to us. They may even mirror our fears back to us.

When we intentionally cultivate divine alignment, we grow, shift and evolve. Some of the situations and even some of the people that were a part of your world before may no longer hold the same attraction or appeal. You might even encounter resistance on the part of others to the positive changes that you're making in your life. People may become uncomfortable with who you're becoming. On a very deep level, your moving forward may cause them to look at the fact they have, somehow, chosen what they are experiencing. They may feel like they are losing you. Your changing will be a huge "wake up" call for them. On some level they will most likely realize that they have the choice and freedom to move forward in their lives also.

Many people are living...or settling for lives that are not what they actually want. They do this because somewhere, somehow, they have come to believe that they can't have what they really want. They might be afraid of success or of becoming too happy. These are very common fears. They might even believe that they don't deserve goodness. Many people live in a form of self-induced amnesia, pretending that their lives are "doable and ok" when what they have is not the totality of what they want at all.

When you move forward the people around you may temporarily snap out of their "amnesia". Some of them may decide to take your lead and move forward in new, exciting ways also. Some of them may not. Some of them may become so uncomfortable that they try to "unconsciously" sabotage you or hold you back.

Sometimes when we move forward we may find that not everyone we know and love will move forward with us. This is more common than not. It's something that we have to be aware of and prepared for.

People have their own journeys. Sometimes their path will continue on with yours. Sometimes not. This can be difficult to cope with. Sometimes it can even be heartbreaking. It may be challenging for you to realize that in order for you to fully embrace your own highest good you have to let go of others and allow them their own journey. We might imagine that because God is creating change within our lives that God is going to change the people we know and love to make it possible for them to continue to be present in our lives when we have the desire to change and have done the work and they haven't.

When one door closes another one opens.

God loves everyone the same and wants the highest outcome for everyone. Sometimes people make the choice to change, and sometimes they don't, depending on where they are in their lives. Not everyone is intended to journey together throughout life and God respects everyone's choices.

Allow people to travel the journey of their own lives and in the same respect take a stand for yourself. Believe in yourself and respectfully refuse to hold yourself back no matter what is going on or who is involved. Allow yourself to be all you can be. It doesn't matter where you find yourself in your life. You are never too young or too old. Any situation can be changed for the better. Give yourself permission to soar regardless of where you find yourself, who you have surrounded yourself with and what you have believed and experienced in the past.

If you feel trapped, stagnant, or like you are holding yourself back take some time to daydream about the things on your manifesting list. Or just make up a daydream out of the blue that brings you joy. Use your imagination. Where would you like to live? What would you love to be doing that helps you to feel free, joyous and more alive? Spend time creating this beautiful day dream until you feel happiness bubbling up.

Actively maintain your own happiness. You can't do this for anyone else. It's important that everyone learn to do this for themselves. When you create your own joy and satisfaction you solidly learn how to do this under different circumstances and you become an inspiration to others.

In general, people are not used to perpetuating joy and truth. This is something that we must be willing to initiate and sustain ourselves. This is how we show ourselves that we believe in and love ourselves.

There may be people in your life right now who create a lot of drama, are negative or needy. Recognize this and allow yourself to accept that by pursuing your dream you are most likely moving away from them. If they are important to you this may be difficult or unexpected. As people move forward they are constantly having to reevaluate who they spend time with, who drains them and who fills them with joy, who stresses them out and who is uplifting.

Be unafraid in allowing people to go their own way. Be unafraid in moving forward in your own life. Some people live their whole lives without truly scratching the surface of the divine plan. They hold themselves back never allowing themselves to be all they can be.

We all have to make the choice to be happy.

We were not meant to sacrifice our lives and joy for other people. By doing this, we do ourselves and them a disservice. We help everyone and the whole world by adding joy and love to it. We can't do that if we are playing small or acting out roles in order to fit in, or if we have tuned our awareness and sensitivity so far down that we have forgotten that we have the capacity to achieve our dreams and visions. We can get so caught up serving people's agendas, egos or their issues. People can lose an entire life doing that and never reach their own happiness. Instead, make the conscious effort to serve people's divine potential and their alignment.

Allow yourself to be all you can be. By doing this you actually support others in their journey to happiness and fulfillment.

Remember that your journey into greater alignment will bring new friends and relationships. Make an effort to seek out new people to relate to who share your new ideas, aspirations and values. Take classes. Join like-minded groups. Ask the Divine to lead you to new, holistic friendships. This is very important. They will nourish your growth, support you on your journey, give you ideas to succeed and help you create new opportunities to share your gifts. They will surround you with the love and insight that you need to continue your journey through the ups and downs.

Release, embrace and allow.

Lovingly release all that isn't working in your life.
Gain the education.
Forgive and bless where necessary.
Release without judgement and with great love and compassion.

Embrace the changes. Embrace the process. Embrace the extra effort you will have to make in order to stay in alignment. Realize that in following the divine plan of your life you are most likely going to have to be more present and more conscious than you have ever been. Embrace all that is being asked of you in order for you maintain divine alignment. Don't be afraid or daunted by it. It's all a part of the journey.

Allow the blessings to flow to you. Allow the gifts to surge through you. Allow for continual happiness, joy and satisfaction.

Decide to have all of the goodness that God has in store for you. Share your life with the inspiring and uplifting people that the

Divine has brought into your world. Allow yourself to soar. Allow yourself to be happy, fulfilled, successful and loved. Expand your awareness. Make sure that you aren't sabotaging or holding yourself back in any area of your life.

Be watchful, present, aware and joyous.

****

<u>I REFUSE TO HOLD MYSELF BACK. I GIVE MYSELF PERMISSION TO HAVE ALL GOD HAS IN STORE FOR ME AND I ALLOW MYSELF TO BE HAPPY, FULFILLED AND SURROUNDED BY LOVING, EXCITED, SUPPORTIVE FRIENDS.</u>

****

<u>Exercise #23</u>

Take out your journal. Make a list of the people closest to you. Objectively and lovingly look at how your relationship with them functions. Take a look at how any qualities you associate with them reflects on qualities you yourself have.

If these qualities are good, note them. If these qualities are less than desirable, note them and make an effort to heal them within yourself. Look at this as an opportunity to see what is going on within you so that you can evolve and grow. Approaching this exercise with the utmost honesty, awareness, compassion and love will help you to get a clearer sense of yourself.

When you have finished this exercise go deep into your heart and thank everyone on your list for being in your life and for serving as a mirror to you. Say a deep felt "thank you" to them as you acknowledge the gift that they have brought you. This may be difficult to do in some cases where there has been violence or abuse. You may need to work through the "Wisdom Beyond Forgiveness" meditation at the end of this book and on the meditation app.

Be patient and loving with yourself as you go through this exercise. Take the time and space you need to process.

Exercise #23b

Take out your journal. Describe any areas where you may be holding yourself back, places where you could be more fulfilled or where you have noticed problems in your life.

Look at each thing on your list and send love to the situation and yourself. Forgive yourself for allowing the situation to exist in this way. Go deep into meditation and ask for the best way to remedy the situation. Surrender the situation to God.

****

Allow the brilliance of God's love for you to shine through everyone you know and through all you do. No holding back.

CHAPTER 24
EXPECTANCY / DIVINE TIMING

As we step into alignment we learn to expect things to work out for the best. This means moving into the understanding of divine timing and expectancy. Through divine alignment we enter into a co-creative process where we are surrendered to the highest outcome. This also includes the timing of things. When we know that there is a timing for all things and that God has planned everything perfectly we can solidly rest in this. We can expect the best outcome at the right time. We can completely surrender.

Expectancy is a lightness. It's a feeling that involves trust and gratitude. We know for sure that what we are expecting or better is on the way. We can go into deep gratitude before ever seeing it in the physical.

When we go to the store we expect to get there. When we order things online, we expect for them to arrive. When we turn the lights on we expect them to work.

Expectancy touches deeply into our self-esteem and sense of deserving. If we don't feel worthy of receiving, we will have difficulty receiving the best. We will have even more difficulty expecting it.

Divine timing is constant and ongoing. It's all pervasive. Most people aren't aware of it but it's actually happening all of the time. Everything in the natural world is manifesting according to divine timing. When it comes to our own lives, we can get in the way of this and self-sabotage. We have to stay in the energy of knowing that there is a purpose and flow to things working out in a certain way and at a certain time.

There are many things that have to happen in order to make things manifest. Within the time that elapses between getting clear about what we are manifesting and when we finally have manifested our goals, many things will have occurred in order to create the situation. As mentioned before, many times the things that had to change were not only in the outer world but also within us.

Do whatever comes to mind to create the changes within yourself so that you can easily step into your manifestation. Keep raising your frequency and vibration. When you are a perfect match vibrationally for what you are seeking to create, everything can move forward faster.

All of creation takes time and moves through different process in order to manifest. An oak tree takes time to grow from an acorn into a full grown tree. It takes time and many different changes for a child to grow into an adult. Enjoy the process of change and allow yourself the luxury of creating your life step by step, piece by piece. This whole process allows mastery and skill to emerge. Stay in expectancy as you grow and evolve. You'll be surprised at the different things you learn and become involved in as you approach your goals.

As you move in the energy of expectancy you may actually not always receive the result you desired. Continue to follow your intuition in expectancy. You will eventually manifest your dream or better...according to the divine plan. And through all of the experiences you have you'll gain an education that you can use. If you don't initially succeed you will have learned what not to do and you will grow stronger because of it. When you do manifest your goals you will have a road map to help you continue creating positive outcomes. The key is to stay surrendered throughout it all. Within this surrendered state, divine timing emerges unhindered by any interference we may be bringing to the table. In this way expectancy and divine timing work in our favor in ways we may not have originally anticipated.

While you are waiting stay in joyous anticipation and gratitude knowing that it has already happened on some level.

Go deeply into the feeling that it has already happened. It is here, accessible, available and ready for you right now.

****

I EXPECT ALL OF MY HIGHEST GOOD TO COME TO ME IN EASE, IN GRACE AND IN DIVINE TIMING.

****

Exercise #24

Take some time and look at the things you have to do on any given day.

Find a correlating feeling state between having to get things done and the feeling of having finished them.

There are varying levels of expectancy.

Harder things may take more time and effort but they will get done as long as you persist until they are finished.

Look at things that you have already created successfully. Allow yourself to feel good about the fact that you created these things in the right time and in the right way. Revisit how it all came to pass and stay in gratitude around it.

Look at the things on your manifesting list.

Rate them all on a scale of 1-10 in terms of how much you really expect to receive them. You may have a mixture of emotions. You may feel happiness at the thought of receiving… in addition to resistance. You may feel low self-esteem and unworthiness in addition to fear even, yet you know in your heart you truly want the manifestation to occur.

Work with any emotions until you can get clear about staying in expectancy.

Work with any resistance and find the places where you may have difficulty believing and expecting you will receive.

Stay in expectancy about the divine plan manifesting in your life. Completely allow the expectancy of receiving from the Divine to grow within you. This will allow your relationship with God to grow and your consciousness to expand.

****

Expect only the best. Notice the divine timing in your life. It's always perfect.

CHAPTER 25
FAITH / TRUST / PURPOSE

I always say that God has my back 100%. I have complete trust in this.

I relax in this.

I know, God is ultimately responsible for making sure things work out in the highest. I don't have to worry or figure things out. I just stay strong in my faith, take guided action and notice how everything changes around me.

I have had to learn to build faith and trust in the midst of all kinds of challenges and I have become stronger through doing this. I am always aware of the fact that I am in a co-creative process with God. I'm not doing this alone.

I'm also very aware of the purpose behind what I'm doing and my goals. Staying clear about the purpose, and why things have to be a certain way, keeps me focused and sure about my next steps.

I have complete faith in God, and in God's presence in my life. I trust God, and I trust God's love for me.

I embrace my purpose, and the purpose behind what God guides me to do. There are some things I may understand immediately. Other things take more time to understand. I know that I will eventually understand the relevant and important aspects, of any situation.

My faith and trust in God, in my purpose help me to grow stronger in understanding who, and what I am as a divine being.

When manifesting alignment, faith, trust, and purpose help us stay grounded and focused. They keep us strong in the midst of change.

All three work hand in hand creating a fourth quality…certainty. Certainty raises frequency, increases momentum, and expands awareness.

With faith, we gain a deep conviction that things are going to work out positively. With trust, we build confidence; and we feel secure in our decisions and in the process. We move towards our goals with a greater passion, knowing that the Divine is also working on our behalf. We know, regardless of the challenges we face, the end result is always going to be the best, for all concerned. With purpose, we clarify our actions; and we increase our understanding of our goals. We become stronger; and we solidify the conviction, behind why we do what we do.

Why do we want to manifest the things on our list?
Why do we want to manifest a new home? Why do we want a new car?
Why do we want to be in a relationship? Why are we seeking to develop and use our gifts?

Focusing in on the "why" is valuable and important. It keeps things very clear, and keeps you motivated through the challenges inherent in sustaining alignment. It empowers you.

Infusing your purpose with love and gratitude takes it up a step higher.

Worry and stress break up our frequency. They disrupt our capacity to create positive outcomes in a consistent manner. Our vibration drops.

A lot of times, people become daunted and discouraged at the amount of energy and time it takes, to reach their goals. It will take however long it's going to take.

The secret is; to build your trust, keep moving forward, taking daily guided actions in consistency and joy. Don't despair. It is happening; and if you look around, you can see evidence of the changes, versus how things were when you first started. If it's taking longer than you expected, it means that there were more things that had to happen, in order for the whole situation to come together perfectly, and in divine grace. Develop patience. Continue to build your trust and faith. While you are waiting, notice what other things have happened, that enriched your life, that you might not have experienced if you were not on this path. Notice all of the good around you. Notice who and what are now a part of your life that were not in your life before. Allow the journey to unfold and stay present.

While you are waiting, prepare yourself to have your goal. Continue to make yourself increasingly magnetic to all of the things you are seeking. Stay detached and surrendered. Welcome the highest outcome possible.

When we are working towards our goals, God knows what we are really seeking to achieve through the experience. We may feel that only a particular thing, happening in a particular way will help us achieve our goals; but God knows what's best for us, and how this should happen. When we look back, we see how God brought the right people at the right time in order for us to grow, expand, and experience what's best for us. When we notice all of the good that has already happened, it helps us to trust the process and stay inspired.

If you have a lot of stress or if you feel like you are stressed in general begin to cultivate the practice of equanimity and peace. Consider meditating daily. Work to create more joy and balance in your life. The stress and worry will begin to transmute and be absorbed by the higher frequencies. Trust and faith will be easier to maintain, once the stress has been decreased and integrated.

You may face challenges and obstacles. These may be things you have to overcome or lessons that you have to master in order to move forward. Many times obstacles are a blessing in disguise. They're bringing your awareness to something you should know and act on. Maybe it's important for you to consider other aspects of the situation or take a different course of action. Or maybe you need to work through the obstacle, to gain needed experiences or information that will help you, at a later time. Trust that you are; in the right place, in the process, and that things will work out.

When people do finally acquire the situations or relationships they've been seeking, they must be able to hold the energy in order to sustain and maintain the experience. Sometimes if a person hasn't done the inner work, they may unconsciously sabotage the relationship or opportunity; because they haven't prepared themselves for it; and they can't consistently match the frequency of their goals. Trust the different things you are going through, are purposeful, and they will help you hold the energy of your dreams. Trust in your own ability as a divine being to manifest the divine plan.

By building trust in God's love for you, and in your own capacity to manifest your goals, you are growing in self-love, self-awareness and self-empowerment.

Sometimes people may have difficult or negative emotions around their relationship with God. They don't know or trust God.

Perhaps you have chosen to incarnate into a family, that has not embraced the understanding, that there is a God, and God loves and wants only the best for you.

This is very common for the starseed souls.

Some people may need to actively build or rebuild their relationship with God. This is done through engaging and relating to God.

Reach out to God and ask that your perception and emotions towards the Divine be healed.

Sometimes we haven't given much thought to what it means to be a divine being. Many times people don't have a personal reference for this and don't understand that they are holy and have a divine destiny. It may be important to re-frame things in our minds so that we can experience the truth of who and what we are. We may need to create new ideas about how we want to experience our lives, knowing that we are capable and deserving of so much more.

It may take more time and effort than you are aware of for things to manifest but the more you stay in trust and gratitude the better things work out. Keep growing your trust and certainty. Keep remembering your "why". Remember that things have to happen in a particular way for them to be successful. If you plant a seed too early or late in the season, it won't have the proper conditions to really grow so that it can thrive. Success in any endeavor is achieved through taking the right actions with the right attitude and in the right timing. Trust and have faith that everything you are working toward has a divine purpose and that it will come to pass in the highest way to create divine alignment.

****

<u>HOLDING FAST TO MY FAITH, TRUST AND PURPOSE I ACTIVELY USHER IN HEAVEN ON EARTH.</u>

****

<u>Exercise #25</u>

Take out your journal. Write down your purpose for manifesting the things on your list. Get very clear about "why" you want to manifest the things on your list and how this is going to serve you and others.

Write down the ways you are acting in trust and faith.
Write down the ways you may not be.

Work harder to remain in a trusting, faithful attitude.

Trust is believing and taking inspired action regardless of appearances.

Notice where you are surrendered and where you are not. The more awareness you bring to these situations the greater the movement…the more alignment.

****
Clarify Purpose. Maintain faith. Trust God.

CHAPTER 26
GRATITUDE AND JOY

Joy and gratitude, are two of the highest frequency emotions that we can experience. Being able to cultivate and sustain them, will help us to consistently stay in alignment. It's easy to be appreciative and joyous, when things are going well. It isn't as easy to do, when things are challenging; but finding a way to be grateful, even in the midst of difficulty, allows us to the see the bigger picture and expand our awareness. This can give us hope, strength, and energy to transcend and heal situations, as opposed to, feeling victimized and trapped.

Staying in gratitude, allows us to gain a fresh perspective on situations which may normally appear to be negative. We are able to find the gifts in them and move forward, without as much resistance.

Every situation we find ourselves in, has something positive in it. Going deeper into gratitude helps us with acceptance and surrender. It raises the frequency; and through using it, so called negative situations can change into positive ones.

Choose to embrace gratitude and joy throughout your day.

Spend money with gratitude and joy.
Pay your bills with gratitude and joy.
Shop with gratitude and joy.
Walk with gratitude and joy.
Work with gratitude and joy.
Cook with gratitude and joy.
Play with gratitude and joy.
Communicate with gratitude and joy.

Acknowledge and feel your already existing abundance, with gratitude and joy. Doing this will help you to stay aware of all of the goodness, already present, in your life.

Make it a habit to feel gratitude throughout your day. Monitor your feelings closely; so that, if you fall out of gratitude, you can re-establish it. This will help keep your focus in place.

Give yourself permission, to routinely do the things that you enjoy and are grateful for. For some, this may be a whole new way of doing things. It may even bring up some resistance. If this should happen, process the resistance and continue to move forward, in joy and appreciation.

Staying in gratitude and embracing joy, is a way of constantly thanking God and the Divine. Appreciating what we already have, brings us closer to God. It increases the good that is a part of our divine birthright. It brings us more things to appreciate.

Start the moment you open your eyes in the morning. Feel gratitude. Say "Thank you". Take a purposeful breath of air into your lungs. Allow the gratitude to expand as you breathe in. Think of all of the things you have to be grateful for, in that moment. Name as many as you can. Feel and say, "thank you" from the depth of your heart for each one.

As you go through the day, continue this practice in all you do. It's incredibly centering and allows you to remember your blessings. Through staying in gratitude, we are constantly reminded of the miracle of our lives.

Inviting joy and gratitude in showers everything we do with light and divine energy. We become a blessing to ourselves and to the world.

****

<u>I AM JOYOUS, GRATEFUL, AND FULL OF LOVE FOR GOD, FOR MYSELF…AND FOR THE COSMOS.</u>

****

<u>Exercise #26</u>

Pull out your journal. Write down all of the people in your life you are grateful for. Write down all of the blessings in your life that are related to your gifts.

Write down all of the things that make you happy in your life that you are grateful for.

Write down all of the things about your body that you are grateful for…from your lungs moving air in and out of your body, to all of the other ways your body allows you to experience the gifts of life.

After you have spent time writing, go deeply into the feelings in your heart. Spend time with each thing on your list, and feel how deeply appreciative you are for all the blessings in your life.

Allow your heart to open to the energy of gratitude. Imagine the gratitude and joy flowing through your whole body, as you are being present to how thankful you are for all that is happening in your life.

Exercise #26b

On a day where you have free time, do an activity that will bring you joy. Once you finish that activity, move on to another activity that, you know, will bring you joy. Keep going in this way, choosing activities that will bring you joy. Do this the whole day if possible. What you will learn is that you can actually go through the whole day in joy. You will end the day in a higher frequency than you started it on.

****

CHOOSE GRATITUDE. CHOOSE JOY. THESE ARE TWO OF THE FREQUENCIES OF DIVINE ALIGNMENT.*

CHAPTER 27
SELF-LOVE / SELF-RESPECT

The journey of divine alignment, is the journey of love. It's a journey of divine love, unconditional love…self-love. The more we love ourselves, the more we can love God, and others. The more we love ourselves, the more open we are to the divine plan of our lives, the more we can help ourselves stay on track in creating what's best for us.

The healthier our sense of self-esteem, the better we can navigate our lives; because we are able to heal any negative unconscious programming that we may have. We deal with problems that arise through responding to them, as opposed to, being triggered and reacting.

Many people today have difficulty in creating balance. They are accustomed to creating drama and pain, as opposed to, caring for themselves. This is because, they don't understand the value and importance of self-love.

It seems like such a simple and obvious idea. Everything we do for ourselves is based how much we love and respect ourselves. All our beliefs about what is possible and what we feel we deserve, stem from this.

When we love ourselves: unabashedly, without ego or arrogance; just simply, purely, powerfully, and holistically, something majestic and magical happens. Our capacity to allow goodness in expands, and we are healed on many different levels. We become renewed.

Loving yourself is accepting yourself. This is truly the highest frequency we can hold.

Be willing to see the brilliance in yourself. Love all of yourself.

If there are things in your life, or about yourself, that you don't like; make the effort to change them.

Finding a way to love yourself, where you are right now, is the most powerful form of love, and will help you in creating the changes you want to make.

Create practices, around integrating higher levels of happiness and wellness, into your daily routine. Stay in a positive frame of mind, and participate in activities that demonstrate self-care.

As you learn to love, honor, and respect yourself continuously; you will change the nature of what you expose yourself to, and what you are willing to accept in your life.

Are you in relationships, where you are being truly honored for who you are, and for your presence and contribution? Are you honoring yourself and your time in your activities and in your career?

Many times people go into unconscious role playing, especially in family or work situations. Do you respect yourself at all times through your choices; or are you disrespecting yourself, even a little bit, through the people you hang around and/or the activities you participate in?

Self-love grants you an abundance of all things. It affects all areas of your life.

Inversely, any area that is out of alignment with your self-love affects the other areas of your life. For example, perhaps you are in a relationship that is not working. This will affect the other areas of your life, especially if the relationship is negative or abusive.

If you find this is the case, don't be afraid to make the changes needed to restore balance. You can ask God or your higher self, to help you create change in the areas where you are not taking the best care of yourself. Ask God to show you what you need to know in order to understand the bigger picture, around why this is happening.

The more you love yourself, the more love you allow yourself to receive.

Inversely if you are not showing yourself love, you are not in alignment. When this happens, the Divine, will do things to get your attention and help you change, so you will turn towards alignment and show yourself more love. These experiences are not always pleasant. Should this happen, come up with some solutions to move into alignment, and remedy your life before things get worse.

Sometimes the answers are very simple.
Be aware of how much love and respect you are showing yourself.
Change your routines to reflect more self-love where needed.
If there are things in your life that are a drudgery or low frequency, release them from your life or work, to find ways of doing them that creates joy.

As you do, you honor and respect yourself.

Spend time with people who treat you with respect, love, and kindness.

Release anything that is not for your highest good.

Build up to doing only what you are guided to do, and truly enjoy.

Engage in activities that are nourishing to your soul. This increases the alignment in your life.

Self-love is self-respect. And, self-respect means respecting your body, your time, your goals, and your choices. As you respect yourself, you open yourself up to new experiences and a new excitement for life.

Many times we have to develop these higher qualities of self-love, self-esteem, self-care and self-respect. They are all a part of living a balanced life. We need them to move forward in alignment.

****

I HONOR AND VALUE MYSELF. I OFFER MY SELF LOVE, RESPECT, AND GRATITUDE. I ALLOW MYSELF TO RECEIVE THE ABUNDANCE OF THE UNIVERSE AND ALL GOD HAS FOR ME.

****

Exercise #27

Pull out your journal. Take some quiet, undisturbed time and reflect on your life. Look at any places where you are not showing the self-love or respect that you deserve. Be very honest with yourself. List these situations and ask God to help you heal them. Ask your higher self to help you find ways to create balance, so that you can experience more self-worth and self-value, in all areas of your life.

Spend some time in meditation, and be receptive to any ideas that may come to you about honoring and loving yourself more. Brainstorm ways to change things, and then come up with a committed plan to do this.

****
LOVE, HONOR AND RESPECT YOURSELF IN ALL YOU DO. THIS IS THE ESSENCE OF THE DIVINE PLAN.

CHAPTER 28
COMPASSION / KINDNESS

One day, I went to the convenience store to get a cup of coffee. As I was going in the store, a woman was entering before me. I looked her in the eye, held the door, and asked her how her day was. She was stunned. She looked at me and answered. As we spoke briefly, she volunteered to buy my cup of coffee. She went on to say, in that small Midwestern town we lived, no one was particularly courteous to her, or had noticed her in the last three months.

She was grateful that I acknowledged her.

She was a minority, in an area where there were not many people who shared her cultural background. When she shared her story with me, I was deeply touched and wondered, "How can we treat each other this way?"

I personally, make it a point to show kindness and compassion to everyone I meet; throughout the day, whether I know them or not, regardless of any outer differences we may have.

The way we behave and the words we choose, creates a huge impact in our lives and in the world. We can't afford to tune out and pretend that being courteous doesn't matter. With so many people constantly engaging with their phones and computers, we are losing our integrity, our humanity, and our capacity to interact with other people with kindness.

The power of our words and our demeanor is immense. The energy that flows through our body, when we are kind, is high and light. When we don't acknowledge each other or pretend not to see people who are right in front of us; we are cutting ourselves off from our humanity and our divinity.

Throughout many cultures and traditions, people intentionally use words as a creative force. Prayer is an example of this, so are mantras and spiritual songs.

Using our words with insight and care is foundational in creating, our reality and helping other people.

People who constantly criticize, speak negatively, and who use their words carelessly are creating more negativity in their lives. They are adding to the negativity in the world.

Those who use their words wisely and create positive experiences through their words are uplifting and healing the world. They are creating more happiness and joy for everyone to experience.

It has been said; it can take years to nurture a positive relationship and minutes to destroy it, all depending on the words we choose to use.

The power of the spoken word is the power of creation. Words are pure frequency and vibration. It's important to use our words to stay, in alignment, with what we seek to create. We have to watch all of the words we use to make sure, they are kind and supportive.

If we face difficult or challenging situations, learning to change the way we speak and behave can help us, to create peace and balance in our lives. The way we express ourselves can support the highest outcome for all involved...not just us.

This doesn't mean, if something negative happens, we don't speak our truth about it. It means, that we speak with honesty, clarity and compassion. If we use our words to hurt or manipulate people, the universe returns these experiences to us, many times in the most unexpected ways.

In addition, we are not meant to interact with everyone. We have to clearly know who we are meant to engage, and who we are meant to avoid. Just as we must know what situations to engage in, and which ones to avoid. Being kind and compassionate requires awareness, and is not an excuse to be a doormat. We still have to use discretion.

Your demeanor and your words, are powerful tools in creating your reality. Choose them wisely; and infuse them with love, honesty, and integrity. When you are kind, compassionate, and loving, you can change the trajectory of someone else's day… and perhaps their life. Choose to be kind and compassionate. These qualities help usher in Heaven on Earth. This is a great gift that you give yourself, that uplifts everyone you come in contact with.

****

MY COMPASSION, KINDNESS, AND WORDS CARRY A DIVINE POWER. I USE THEM WISELY TO CREATE MY WORLD AND TO SUPPORT POSITIVE CHANGE.

****

Exercise #28

Take time to acknowledge the different people in your life, you may not normally speak to. Give a kind word to the person who is helping you check out at the grocery store, or who is bagging your food. When you pick up your dry cleaning, ask about the person's day as you are paying for your clothes. When calling customer service for any problem, have a friendly tone; and acknowledge the person on the other end by saying, "How are you?" before diving into the reason you called.

At the end of every encounter, remember to say, "Have a good day." All these people have been instrumental in making your day run smoother. In this way, you are intending for happiness to reach them too.

As we work to create greater happiness, it's important to share it with others. Happiness is what we are all seeking. As we spread it to others, we are creating the energetic circuit that brings it back to us.

Exercise #28b

Take some time to look at different situations and people in your life. Where could you be kinder and more compassionate? As you look at the scenarios, come up with new ideas and ways to deal with the situations, that will allow the highest outcome for all concerned. You can even create some positive scripts and run through ideas, before you actually see the people. If you have a situation with a relative or a co-worker, where there is agitation, take some time before seeing them, and come up with ways to deal with this; that will allow you to stay in the highest frequency, during the time you interact with them. You can send love to them and to the interaction, before you have to see them. You can visualize a positive outcome. This will allow the situation to shift. If you have been kind and compassionate and there is still agitation, it may be a message from the Divine that you are not meant to interact in the same way with this person, or with a particular situation.

When we choose to act compassionately and use our words wisely, we are taking greater responsibility for ourselves, and others. Choosing to be compassionate and kind, is the key to changing our lives; and create greater well-being on the planet.

****
KINDNESS AND COMPASSION ALLOW THE DIVINE TO SHINE THROUGH YOU.

CHAPTER 29
SURRENDER / FORGIVENESS

The divine plan of your life happens through surrender.

When we surrender, we allow God to create the outcomes. This may not be an easy concept to grasp. In the long run, it's the one thing that has to happen for the divine plan to unfold, in the way God has planned it.

My journey of surrender has taken many unexpected twists and turns. When I finished meditating for four years, I went to Belize. In Belize, I continued to grow and evolve. All the same, I faced a period of time where I had no food for 21 days.

I said to God… "I haven't eaten in 21 days. Someone must come and feed me." I then completely surrendered the outcome.

Within an hour, someone approached me and gave me $50 Belize dollars. I was able to eat, and my life took a different turn after that.

This was a complete act of surrender. I had no idea of how it was going to happen. I only knew that I was doing everything that I could to stay in alignment and that it was important for me to eat. In releasing it to God, I allowed God to bring the answer to me.

Surrender, allows us to experience God's presence and God's answers. It allows us to see the nature of how God cares for us. It's profoundly transformational.

Surrender and forgiveness are a part of our evolutionary process. On a daily basis, we are faced with situations which call to us to surrender, and take action based on what we feel God is guiding us to do. In the same respect, we have to stay in a deep state of acceptance and forgiveness, of ourselves and others. This keeps us in a flow, where we are present to what is happening around us; and yet, we aren't blocked by resistance and negativity.

I surrender all of the aspects of my life to God daily.

What I know is, through surrender I access divine alignment which is always available for me. Should I ever go out of alignment, even a little bit, I surrender even more. I gain the insights that God wants me to understand; and then, I act on it. I am completely committed to this process.

Staying in a state of continual forgiveness is also just as important. Forgiveness is a master frequency which dissolves, blocks, and resentment. It helps us release judgement; and it allows divine energy to flow, through our being and through our affairs. Our bodies become hardened, and we can even make ourselves sick when we don't forgive. We can't access the highest guidance, if we are unforgiving. Being able to release any resentment, judgement, and/or anger through forgiveness is imperative. Inversely, what we are truly seeking many times is to be forgiven. We are the creators of our lives. We have been the ones to set into motion or condoned, the different dramas and situations that are affecting us. Through forgiving ourselves and others, we create a complete circuit where we are in a fully surrendered state. We release the energies which would harm us and create imbalance. We allow ourselves to be forgiven and restored.

I have an exercise included in the back of the book called "Wisdom Beyond Forgiveness". This exercise allows you to flood the timeline, of any negative event, with unconditional love. Doing this changes the energy of the event, freeing you and all involved, helping you to gain the needed information and wisdom. The reason it's called "Wisdom Beyond Forgiveness" is because, when we work at such high levels to heal situations we have to move through the forgiveness stage, release any resistance, and allow ourselves to grow. The wisdom gained allows us to see the lesson in the experience, and gain the blessings from it. We understand how powerful we are in sending unconditional love. We begin to experience our capacity to heal and affect all outcomes and situations; including, healing the energy around things that have happened in the past. Going through the experience helped us to become the person we are today. Accessing the wisdom beyond forgiveness, allows us to emerge stronger and more aligned with God.

I have also included two prayers below which help create healing and balance, through forgiveness. They are prayers that clear any energy or esoteric transference, from any other lifetimes that have been brought into this one. These could be specific, to different situations or people. If you have created anything in a past life that needs to be forgiven, these are extremely helpful.

So many people have difficulty trusting the process of surrender. They have problems forgiving others, and allowing themselves to be forgiven. Be loving and compassionate to yourself, if you have problems in these areas. Work through them with consistency and love.

Stepping into alignment is moving forward with a surrendered and forgiving heart. It all goes hand in hand.

****

<u>I ALLOW FORGIVENESS, SURRENDER AND UNCONDITIONAL LOVE INTO MY LIFE.</u>

****

<u>Exercise #29</u>

Take out your journal and make a list of the situations in your life where you may not be surrendered. Write down the areas that need forgiveness. Go through each situation, on the list, and practice surrendering it to God, as much as you can. This exercise may be more of a process. You may be able to surrender some of the situations to God today. On another occasion you may be able to surrender more. Continue to revisit your list until you feel that you are fully surrendered, forgiving and complete with the process.

Depending on the nature of the situations you are working on, you may also want to ask God to help create the surrender, healing, and forgiveness. It's important to seek divine assistance if you are having problems.

You may want to listen to the "Wisdom Beyond Forgiveness", the "Releasing Regret Energy" and the "24 Heart Chakra Release" meditations daily if you have any stuck energy around forgiveness and regret.

You may also want to seek the help of a skilled energy practitioner, or join one of our group calls.

****

Prayer to Release Any Cellular Memory Or Esoteric Transference From Any Past Life

(Say 3x or 9x to activate the sacred power of numbers within the prayer.)

I am of God.
I ground myself to the Earth.

I come before you, God, for forgiveness for anything I have done in any past life, to infinitum, through all space/time continuum in any dimension, that has been brought back into this lifetime and is affecting me now.

I release it all to you, God, with unconditional love.

I thank you, God, and I send you my unconditional love.
So be It / Amen

Prayer To Release Past Life Connection Issues

(Say 3x or 9x to activate the sacred power of numbers within the prayer.)

I am of God.
I ground myself to the Earth.

I come before you, God, for forgiveness for anything I have done in any past life, through infinitum, through all space and time that has been brought back into this dimension, and is affecting my relationship with (name specific person) now.

I release it all to you, God, with unconditional love.

I thank you, God, and send you my unconditional love.
So Be It / Amen

****

IN A FULLY SURRENDERED AND FORGIVING WORLD ALL THINGS ARE POSSIBLE.

CHAPTER 30
TO ALIGN OR NOT TO ALIGN /
THAT IS THE QUESTION

Our lives reflect, whether or not we are in alignment.

Alignment is both inner and outer, and on every level. Making an effort to create inner alignment, as well as, outer alignment helps create balance. There may be certain aspects of your life that are more in alignment, than others. For instance, you may be good at surrounding yourself with supportive friends, but you may experience a lot of worry and stress. As we approach intentionally aligning ourselves and our lives with the divine plan, it's important to take an honest look at where we are in alignment, and where we are not.

Noting where we are out of alignment in our lives, and within ourselves, may be uncomfortable and even painful. No one intentionally sets out to create situations that will work against them. All the same, being able to take the first step and look at how aligned your life is, can be a huge eye opener in helping you to restructure; and heal the different areas in your life that could be working better.

Inner alignment is about balancing out the thoughts, feelings, and emotions. It's about clarifying your commitment to your dreams and desires. It's about transmuting and healing, any conflicting subconscious beliefs and stories. It's about staying motivated to take inspired action. All of this, is the foundation of creating alignment in our world. Inner to outer. As above, so below. The clearer we are internally, the better we can care for ourselves externally.

God and your soul, are in loving constant awareness, of how you are living your life. At the same time, the nature of what you are supposed to be doing with your life, changes in an ongoing way. There are some things, that are more in alignment for you at different times in your life. At other times, it may be totally out of alignment to do these same exact things.

The Divine, will give you cues when you are not in alignment. When you are in alignment, things will move along in a particular flow. You will know. There may be challenges, but these challenges exist to evolve you. When you are out of alignment, your frequency will not be in the highest. In addition, things may go wrong in ways that you can't ignore. This is your soul's way of getting your attention. If you are seeking alignment, but you are not heeding the signals from the Divine, things will continue to escalate in a negative way; and bigger wake up calls will happen. These, wake up calls, happen to help you understand that you are out of alignment, and you need to change things. These wake up calls are not pleasant. In my case, I ended up losing everything. This, was the biggest wakeup call of all. From there, I began to really understand that when you are in alignment things get better, and when you are not they get worse.

On top of that, the Divine will do things, in an unmistakable way, to get your attention. You may be on a path that is out of alignment, which is stressful enough; on top of that, something extremely unpleasant may happen to wake you up.

It's not that, God, will send you negativity; it's that your soul is seeking to get your attention because, it's important to change courses. It does this in the most effective way it can, with complete love and compassion. It does this to create more self-love and self-care within you.

Heed any incidents, that may happen to wake you up, as gifts from the Divine. Let yourself embrace the conversations that your soul is initiating with you, about what is best for you. When these things happen, acknowledge them. Use them. Gain wisdom from them. Go into gratitude about them. Take them and create something better, from them. Stay surrendered, and call on God to help you understand the best way to move forward.

Take consistent guided action. Guided action moves us out of our comfort zones, and into places we have never been before. This is good. We can't create alignment by staying where we are, after making the commitment to change. We step into alignment by taking consistent actions; moving us into, totally different and many times, unfamiliar experiences.

Sometimes people are uncomfortable with all of the changes. They settle back into "the known" even though "the known" is, in many instances, out of alignment. Any change can be stressful, even positive change. Love yourself. Pamper yourself; and step back into alignment again, and again, and again. It's an ongoing and ever evolving, process.

Accept that you may experience some discomfort as you move into greater alignment. You may become very uncomfortable as you leave behind your "former way of being", ie., your comfort zone, in order to embrace who, you are becoming. This is all a part of the process. As you continue to access greater alignment, you will become used to the nature of the "discomfort of change" as a part of the process, and associate it with positive forward movement.

The more you take consistent steps in the direction of alignment, the better your life will get. My life is living proof of this. I can say wholeheartedly, if I can do this you can also.

****

MY SOUL IS EVER WATCHFUL, SEEKING ONLY THE HIGHEST AND MOST DIVINELY ALIGNED EXPERIENCES.

****

Exercise #30

Use your journal to note any experiences, in your life, that are clearly signaling that you are out of alignment. Look at the areas that could use improvement. Go into meditation; and ask the Divine or your soul, for guidance and help, in creating balance and greater alignment. Take the steps to make those changes in a timely way; and show yourself and the universe, that you are loving and caring towards yourself.

Consistently working to create alignment, builds a muscle in learning how to maintain alignment. Every positive step carries you forward.

****
TO STAY IN ALIGNMENT IS TO ACHIEVE THE DIVINE PLAN FOR YOUR LIFE.

CHAPTER 31
STEPPING INTO LOVING AUTHORITY / COMMANDING YOUR LIFE INTO ALIGNMENT

I have come into the world with a purpose. I have come to be an example to others and to serve. I have been trusted with the power to heal. I have been trusted with the power to teach people about themselves. One of the most important things, is to be able to say, "I use my gifts completely and wisely." I learn more, and more about what this means, on a daily basis.

An important part of how I fulfill my purpose, is through enlisting divine assistance.

Through communing with the Divine, I've learned how to structure my requests as a command. Most people have been taught to be subservient, and to feel undeserving in their relationship with God. Taking authority in your life, and commanding the Divine Realm to assist you in healing; and creating your life has nothing to do with being reverent towards God. I am extremely reverent and grateful for the Divine. This is the most important part of my life.

But in order to truly function in the role that I came here to assume, I have to step into my divine authority. I have to command my life into order. By commanding the angels and the Divine, I become very clear about what has to happen; and I take my place as a divine being.

When a person begins to command their life into authority they grow in their self-esteem and personal power, not in an arrogant or self-centered way, but in a grounded and purposeful way. Most people are not used to being in command of their lives. Worthiness issues, which affect so many, dissolve when a person steps into loving authority in their lives.

This is a huge, important aspect in reclaiming one's birthright, and in accessing humanity's original blueprint.

We are divine beings created to be the Ultimate Being; and our inception ushered in a new addition to the cosmos, which had never been seen before. We were created to expand God's vision and to be a vessel of God's will. We were given free will, not to use it against ourselves or to destroy our lives; but because, we are the children of God; and God wanted to give us creative freedom.

With the fall of humanity, we lost sight of the fact that, God, only uses power within the framework of unconditional love. Humanity has fallen so far away from its original state; that today, most people don't have the capacity to think about, and/or comprehend, what we were in our original state.

In reclaiming our divine birthright, we have to step back into authority in our lives.

I have included a section of the sacred prayers that I have been gifted, from the divine realm. I use them constantly throughout the day; and they are, one of the most, potent and powerful ways to create change that I have found. They can help you awaken your divine nature. Through using them, you get a sense of how to proceed in different areas of your life.

The more you take command of your life, the more your personal power grows. The more you become who you were destined to be, the greater your potential for good will expand and impact, the planet and humanity. You become a conscious steward of your life. You become an example to help others awaken and align.

Take command of your life. It's a gift from God. Be fearless, compassionate, and loving. The universe will unfold before you.

****

I COMMAND MY LIFE INTO ORDER.

****

<u>Exercise #31</u>

Look through the sacred prayers at the end of the book. Find at least one that you feel comfortable in using on a daily basis. Commit to using it every day. Say it with authority and power.

Begin to look at different areas of your life that may need attention. Approach the healing of these parts of your life, with the full authority that you have been given by God. Through stepping into authority, using kind, compassionate, and consistent application you can change any and all situations in your life.

****

YOU WERE CREATED TO COMMAND AND EXPAND THE COSMOS THROUGH LOVE AND KINDNESS. STEP INTO YOUR AUTHORITY.

CHAPTER 32
TIME / TIMELINES / SOUL FAMILIES

Many people assume that time is localized and only travels in one direction; forwards. Quantum physics has proven time flows forwards and backwards, and that there are multiple dimensions where time also exists.

The multi-faceted aspect of time is compounded by the fact that, in a true scientific sense, there is no time or space at all. Everything exists within this present moment, that we call the "now". This "now" is so complex and vast, that most people cannot comprehend it. There are people known as adepts (usually found within the spiritual traditions, especially within the esoteric branches of yoga) who have, through intense, personal work been able to raise their frequency and vibration, high enough to break through the perception; they only exist in one lifetime and in one dimension, at any given time.

My personal experience is, we have had many different lifetimes; and that, we exist in different dimensions at the same time. We're experiencing past, present, and future timelines simultaneously;

even though, the mind is typically only perceiving one timeline, our current one.

Our capacity to achieve our goals, may be deeply affected by these different timelines. In many cases, there can be some bleeding over from one timeline to another, especially in regards to past timelines. Our past lives have influenced and shaped our current reality; in the same way, who we were years ago plays a part in who we are today. We are affected by other life times and experiences; we usually don't even remember.

The veils between the different lifetimes is very thin right now. Because of this, many things are being transferred through the timelines, which wouldn't normally be transferred. There may be particular traumas or experiences, that were so powerful, they somehow followed us into this life.

We have to stay strong and aware so that we can discern the meaning and purpose of different situations around us. Are the origins of the situation from our current life or from a past life? In either case, the way we heal it is the same, through love, compassion and dedication. The importance here lies in the fact that if we create imbalance anywhere…even in another lifetime, we must take responsibility and heal the situation.

Sometimes we need to have a piece of information from another lifetime that's important. At the right time, we will receive the pertinent information from the Divine about what happened in the past in order to help us integrate and resolve particular situations.

We can send love into the past. We can send love into the future. We can immerse ourselves in acceptance and unconditional love right now. This creates profound change.

There are people who come into our lives that have past life connections with us. There are groups of souls that have known each other and worked together in different lifetimes. Many times people have worked on a common cause with a goal to manifest. These groups of people are like soul families. Typically, the connection that we have with these people from other lifetimes is very powerful and strong. Recognizing that we have a soul level connection with these other people and allowing ourselves to see what God wants to do through these groups helps move into even greater levels of alignment. These soul families can offer a lot of support and love. As we look at what brings us joy they may be a part of what we came here to do and we may also be a part of what they came to do. Ultimately soul families are here to increase the joy and to work in partnership.

In some cases, we may have brought in unresolved issues with the people in our lives. We may need to do some clearing around this to rebalance any residual energies that are affecting our lives and theirs. If we have any issues with them that need to be cleared up, we can use the prayers at the end of this chapter to heal them.

We can also use the prayers below for any esoteric transference that has leaked from other lifetimes into this one. These energetic transferences come from other places and times and the original causes may be unrecognizable to us in our current incarnation, and yet we are still dealing with them energetically even though we may not understand the nature of this dynamic in our lives. In other words, we may be experiencing imbalances in our life that originated in another lifetime. In order to fully heal this situation or pattern we still have to do the inner work. The prayers listed below work through forgiveness, surrender and allowing God to create the changes that are to be made.

In addition, many people are experiencing blocks in their lives that were put there by negative influences. These problems were purposefully put in place to stop people from living on the divine timeline of their lives.

The negative influences/energies ultimately can't stop you from living on the divine timeline but they can distract, interfere, block and discourage you.

These negative interferences cause people to go off on alternate timelines that aren't in the highest and best. People haven't been educated about this. Because they don't know that this is happening, they don't work to prevent or rectify it. And so when blocked from accessing the divine timeline, they get discouraged and go off on other timelines never understanding how they have been manipulated.

There are an infinite number of timelines that anyone could access at any moment. In the same way, there are an infinite number of choices that access these different timelines. Through using our intuition, prayer and meditation we can discern if we are on the divine timeline of our lives.

If you feel that you have been blocked from being on your divine timeline, you can clear this through spending time with God or your soul. Ask God to clear all the blocks preventing you from accessing your divine timeline. This will open up the pathways to your divine timeline for you in the present and make it easier for you to attain alignment.

We may wonder how we could possibly be blocked from being on the divine timeline of our lives if God created it for us to experience. When we step out of alignment through our thoughts, deeds and feelings we lower our frequency and vibration and we make ourselves susceptible to being manipulated and violated. Doing this, we enter into a space where all kinds of other energies have access to us and feed off our energy. These negative energies work to create situations to drive a person's frequency down so that they can continue to feed off of, manipulate and control a person's life.

As mentioned earlier, there are remote viewers and negative entities that manipulate and violate people in order to drain them of energy. The question might be why would God let this happen?

God didn't let these things happen.

We are the ones choosing to participate in these things through the frequency and vibration we hold. We all have free will to choose what we experience. God is simply honoring our choices. We are divine beings and have had complete and total say in our lives the whole time.

Anything can be changed at any point in our lives. We have to choose to turn things around. We must take greater responsibility in our lives in order to access the divine timeline. Spend more time communing with God. Keep your frequency high. Heal the places in your life where you have been manipulated or blocked.

We have created an Akashic Records clearing meditation that clears any blocks or tampering which may have been recorded within the Akashic records, which is the universal database of all of humanity's thoughts, words and deeds. Clearing the places where you experienced tampering allows you to have access to the options which were being blocked. Your present moment will clear up considerably and you will find it easier to access your divine timeline.

Our experience is more comprehensive than this one life. And because all of our lifetimes are flowing in a continuum we may want to take a step back and view it all from a much wider perspective. If we create something that harms us in one lifetime we will have to take responsibility for it, restore and rebalance it eventually.

We are responsible for healing all of the circumstances and any damage that was caused when we stepped out of alignment. This is a wonderful gift because we get to see how capable and powerful we are in creating goodness, joy, success and harmony. We grow stronger and more aware. We expand and experience our own wholeness and our own holiness.

Restoring ourselves is not always a fast, easy or simple process but it is always the most important and best thing we could ever do.

In the same respect, I have had people ask me if suicide is a divine option that allows people to escape their problems and return back to Heaven faster. I tell them that this is absolutely a false idea planted into people's minds. If a person takes their own life they will have to come back in the next life and heal the damage done and/or face what they were seeking to originally escape. This is a classroom. We are here to master the experiences our soul has chosen so that we can fully evolve and realize ourselves as the divine beings that we are.

The more we evolve through our deep inner work, the more we will be able to understand the nature of time and our existence here and on different timelines. It is a natural process that occurs through our spiritual growth. We begin to recognize the truth of our immortal souls. The deeper we go into divine alignment as we discover more about ourselves.

As we journey into our own divinity, the limitations of time and space fall away. We begin to remember that we are immortal beings and that time is a construct that can never control or limit us. It is illusional and malleable in nature. Because of this, we can use it to our advantage. As we emerge through our practices and step into divine alignment, we realize the divine within us is greater than any problem we could face and that all of our challenges exist only to encourage us further into alignment and to give us needed wisdom. We master our experiences and free ourselves from limitation.

****
I AM AN ETERNAL, DIVINE BEING. ALL TIME AND SPACE SERVE TO HELP ME.
****

Exercise #32

This is an exercise to expand consciousness. Take some quiet time and reflect on any places or past eras which seem familiar to you or which have always held an interest. Ask God to reveal any past lives that hold a particular relevance to the current life you are in right now. Ask to be shown how these lives have impacted your current life and how information from the other lives can help you in this one. As you gain insight allow the information to help you become more centered and determined.

Exercise #32b

Pull out your journal. Make a note of all of the people you feel may be in your soul group or soul family. You will know these people through the depth of your connectedness to them and the activities that you do together. Spend some time feeling into any recollection of other places and times that you know them from. Enjoy the process and play with it. Recognize the immortality of life and remember that you have come with others to enjoy community, build your lives together, share your gifts and restore Heaven on Earth.

Exercise #32c

Look back over your life. Using your journal, make notes as to where you may have been manipulated through ignorance, fear or different emotions into making choices that were not in your highest good. Many times this is how we would experience a block to moving forward. Look at your gifts. Look at your relationships. Look at your home life. Get a sense or feeling about the levels of alignment present in the different areas in your life. If you feel there could have been any manipulations/violations or blocks in any of these areas, spend some time with God and ask God to clear them all so that you can access the divine timeline of your life without any interferences.

****

Prayer to Release Any Cellular Memory Or Esoteric Transference From Any Past Life

(Say 3x or 9x to activate the sacred power of numbers within the prayer.)

I am of God.
I ground myself to the Earth.

I come before you God for forgiveness for anything I have done in any past life to infinitum, through all space/time continuum in any dimension that has been brought back into this lifetime and is affecting me now.

I release it all to you God with unconditional love.

I thank you God and I send you my unconditional love.
So be It / Amen

Prayer To Release Past Life Connection Issues

(Say 3x or 9x to activate the sacred power of numbers within the prayer.)

I am of God.
I ground myself to the Earth.

I come before you God for forgiveness for anything I have done in any past life through infinitum, through all space and time in any dimension that has been brought back into this dimension and is affecting my relationship with (name specific person) now.

I release it all to you God with unconditional love.

I thank you God and send you my unconditional love.
So Be It / Amen

****
You are an immortal being of love and light. Expand into your truth and become all that you are.

CHAPTER 33
MANIFESTING VIBRANT HEALTH / PERFECT RELATIONSHIPS / ABUNDANCE AND SUCCESS

Once, I had three different clients who came to me, all around the same period of time, all ladies. Each one of them wanted to meet, and have a relationship with their soulmate. I told each one that it was not for me to manifest a soulmate for them; but what I could do, was help them reach the vibration of a soulmate relationship. I worked with each of them separately, one-on-one, for weeks to help raise their frequency and keep their energy balanced. After we finished our sessions together, each one of them met and entered into a relationship, with wonderful men. Each one of the ladies, felt the partner they had attracted was exactly what they had been working towards, their soulmate.

Everything that we are working towards achieving, can be viewed the same way. These ladies held the idea of what they were working towards, but we targeted a specific frequency in order match the soulmate relationship. Knowing that a successful career has a certain frequency; and that, vibrant health has a certain frequency; we can also use the same basic idea to introduce the matching frequency, into our lives. Understanding with certainty, that God, wants these things for us, and has given us these things, in the divine plan of our lives, helps; because we realize that it has already been created on another level; and that, God supports us. What we want is waiting for us to access it.

In order to access this plan and allow it to come into fruition, we have to access the frequency and vibration that matches all of the things waiting for us.

The perfect, new home has a particular frequency. The health of all of our family members, also a particular frequency.

The body already has a divine blueprint, which allows it to access vibrant health, through aligning to the corresponding frequency. All of the cells in the body are intelligent. They are responding to our thoughts, intentions, emotions, and frequency. They know how to manifest perfect health in the body. As we raise our frequency, and release the idea of vibrant health; through our imagination, the cells of our body resonate, in alignment, to the feelings and frequency that we are holding. They can self-correct and do the healing themselves.

Everything in creation is designed, similarly, to respond to the frequency we are holding. Our gifts have a frequency. Using our gifts has a certain frequency.

If we can work to attain the highest frequency and vibration; the journey will be easier because all of the things, that we are seeking to create, are within the highest frequency of creation.

As mentioned before, sometimes we have a lot of things to work through in our lives. There could be many things to process and integrate, from our past and within the subconscious, that are creating non-productive outcomes.

No matter what you are going through, and no matter where you start your journey into divine alignment, stay encouraged. Remember, life always supports us in our evolution.

My own personal journey has been one of massive transformation. I have experienced a period when I was out of alignment. I have watched my life fall apart despite my best efforts, at the time, to keep it in place. I now know, God caused all of this to happen, as a way, to awaken me to the fact that I was not living in alignment. I surrendered, and I made the changes according to my inner guidance; and in doing this, my life changed. It didn't happen overnight, but it did happen. I believe, who I have become is the person God intended me to be. I am helping people all over the world through using my gifts; and I know, in the depth of my being, that this is what God wants.

What I know now, everything I am guided to create and manifest, springs from one thing; God's love for me. Everything I am guided to offer out to the world, springs from one thing; God's love for humanity, and Mother Earth. When I stay in alignment with this knowing, everything is easier. Life is joyous and free.

Allowing yourself to open up, and embody the frequency of God's love for you, will create a shift that will expand your consciousness and help you evolve. Divine alignment and the divine plan of your life, will flow effortlessly from this.

God's unconditional love is the highest frequency of all.

Allow it in. Bathe in it. It is what we have all longed for, and the one thing that ultimately changes everything.

****
TRUE AND LASTING CHANGES ARE CREATED THROUGH THE FREQUENCY OF UNCONDITIONAL LOVE.
****

Exercise #33

Pull out your journal.

Set your intention on raising your frequency to that of unconditional love.

List the places in your life where you are experiencing unconditional love.

Go into meditation and visualize what life would look like if you were experiencing unconditional love in all areas of your life.

Write about what life would look like if you were experiencing unconditional love in all areas in your life.

Reach out to your soul and higher self. Ask them to inform and guide you how to create through the energy of unconditional love.

As you keep a record of all of the transformations that are happening in your life through embracing unconditional love you will gain new insights and have "ah-ha" moments that you might not notice if you weren't journaling.

****
* Your life was created to be a blessing, not only to yourself, but to the whole world. Embrace your divinity. You are magnificent.*

CHAPTER 34
YOU DESERVE THE BEST

In the award winning documentary, "I AM", Hollywood producer/director/ filmmaker, Tom Shadyac, goes through an inner transformation which leads him on a journey to the great spiritual teachers, and healers of the world. He asks them two questions: "What's wrong with the world?" and "What's the solution to healing the world?". In both cases, he finds the answer is, the same, "I AM".

We are the ones, who are, creating the problems; and we will solve them.

In the film, Tom reveals his own personal journey.

He recounts a memorable moment, when moving from one huge mansion, to the next. He realizes that this next move, ideally, should have made him happy; but it didn't. Bigger, and better, is how we're conditioned to think; but in the depths of Tom's being, he realized there was no happiness in this, at all.

He later had a life threatening accident; and while, in the midst of his recovery, he decided to change everything, in his life, to reflect his deepest values. He went on a journey to document the truth, as he understood it. The result, is one of the most revealing, and transformational, documentaries ever made, "I AM".

Tom made a lot of changes; in order to, create a life that reflects his inner truth, and joy. He now lives, in a modest home, in a seaside community that shares his values. Instead of limos and private drivers, he bikes to work. These changes were healing to his soul. He is happy now. He shares his story, so that people will: have a reference point; and understand, what it means, to honor your deepest truth; in the midst of, creating abundance and success.

There are many things, we have been conditioned to think we need, or want; but they don't really bring greater happiness. There are ways we are taught to relate, to each other; but they only create more confusion. In the end, no one is truly happy.

One thing I have had to accept, in my journey, is that I deserve the best. Having the best, doesn't mean; I have to spend a lot of money, and live in an ostentatious way. It also, doesn't mean; I am better than anyone else. It means, understanding what truly makes me happy, allowing myself to have it, and realizing that everyone deserves the best.

In my journey of divine alignment, from Bentleys and huge salaries, into the depths of homelessness; and now, into true success and happiness. I have had to learn, to understand, what was right for me and what was not. At one point, I was financially successful; but I had worthiness issues where I did not, and could not, allow in what was really good for me. I was in a cycle of creating "lack of…".

So many people have these issues today, that it's nearly epidemic.

I had to break through the societal conditioning to see God's ways, of doing and seeing things.

The societal conditioning, is driven by a feeling of separation, from God; the self-destructive energy of low self-esteem, and out of control consumerism. Underneath all of this, however, is another blueprint for life that makes sense. It is based upon God's plan and the things in this book.

As mentioned earlier, in this society money is important. It's how we pay for things and live. But it's not, and should not be, the driving force underneath how we feel about ourselves; or how we treat each other. We should use it to create positive change in the world, and to reflect our deepest values.

We all deserve the very best. This is the divine plan for everyone. We all can be financially abundant, really enjoy our lives, and be in service.

In my case, I now live in the American heartland. I love nature, and I love the peaceful life in a small town. I have a wonderful home and family. I cherish my wife and kids. These are the things that make me truly happy. I surround myself with loving people who appreciate life, and have solid values. When it comes to the things that I buy, I always look for the very best quality; but I also seek to support small businesses. I like working with, and empowering, people in their service to the world.

I don't need ostentatiousness, but I do need what's best for me. It's important for me to give this to myself.

It's also important, for me, to use my time and money to help other people.

Healing any worthiness and "lack of" issues, you may have, is important in order to access, and live, the divine plan of your life.

Give yourself permission to have what is best for you.

What will make you truly happy? What will make your heart sing, and fills you with energy and joy, is the very best for you.

God wants the very best for you and what will make you truly happy.

****

<u>GOD HAS CREATED A PLAN FOR MY LIFE FILLED WITH HAPPINESS, AND THE VERY BEST. I ALIGN AND ALLOW IT TO MANIFEST.</u>

****

Exercise #34

Using your journal, make a list of some things that are right for you.
Using your discernment, make sure that these things are honestly the best, as opposed to, things that you want because of conditioning; or because, someone else said they are right for you.

Write out next to each thing why it makes you happy.

Feel deeply, inside of you, your level of awareness and acceptance. Process any resistance, and allow God's love to create the best in your life.

****
*YOU DESERVE THE VERY BEST. IT HAS ALWAYS BEEN THIS WAY. IT WILL ALWAYS BE THIS WAY. LOVINGLY EMBRACE IT.

CHAPTER 35
ALIGNMENT OF THE HEART

Most people understand how important the heart is, in terms of our physical health. What hasn't been so obvious, is that the heart is central in the creative/manifesting process also. Our hearts create the frequency which influences the world around us, and assists us in manifesting alignment and the divine plan.

The work of Gregg *Braden, the* Heartmath Institute, scientists, and doctors in the field, has uncovered key elements about the heart, and the environment we live in. They are providing scientific evidence about the nature and power of the heart, interacting and creating through the energy of the world.

Many ancient texts and doctrines, speak about a technique of maintaining a state of feeling that creates the world around us.

"Ask and it is given; as you ask, believe that you have it." is the paraphrase, of the wisdom, from different traditions.

As modern science is beginning to understand the "how and why"s of this phenomenon, we are seeing a huge surge in the manifesting movement. Consciousness is awakening within people, at the same time, we now have access to information which explains, not only, how the mechanical process of manifestation occurs; but how, we can create the world around us with greater ease than was previously thought.

The heart is the physical organ which helps us to do this.

As mentioned earlier, the whole cosmos is filled with energy and light, from photons and atoms. This energy and light is electrical and magnetic, or electromagnetic in nature.

There is no coincidence, the heart generates an electromagnetic field that is stronger than any other organ in the body.

The electrical field of the heart is hundreds of times stronger, than the electrical field of the mind. The magnetic field of the heart, is thousands of times stronger, than the magnetic field of the mind. In addition, the human heart generates a field of energy, around the body, that some scientists have estimated to extend several feet around the body, perhaps more. It's connected to, and a part of, the biofield.

What we now understand is, the electromagnetic field generated by the heart is influenced and colored, by our thoughts and feelings. Whatever we are thinking or feeling, is sent out in the form of energy information; in which, creates our reality, through influencing the atomic structure, and energy field in the world around us. Again, when we influence the field, we directly influence the structure of the atoms in the field.

In the past science has reported that atoms are 99.9999…% empty space. We now understand, empty space is, actually, not empty. It's filled with electromagnetic energy and light photons. It's filled with consciousness. The energy within the atoms is alive and aware.

The light and electromagnetic energy, within the atom; and the energetic field, surrounding it, is constantly responding to: feelings and intentions, held within the light; and electromagnetic energy, coming from us. Our energy information is giving it direction on what shape to take, and what to do.

This is why, the world is mirroring back to us what we are thinking and feeling. This is why, our beliefs are foundational in creating our world.

This explains why, it's so important to understand what is going on within us; so that, we can purposefully and intentionally create the world around us.

Braeden, refers to this process as an "inner technology" that revolves around intentionally, using our hearts. Our hearts contain 40,000 neurites, or little brain cells, that can think, learn, remember, feel, and communicate independently of the brain. These heart neurites, when working in unison with the brain, create a brain heart connection that is powerful, and unique to humanity. Braden, calls this the marrying of the heart and brain, also known as the extended neural network. This is why we can feel compassion, empathy, intuition and create in the way we do, through thinking and feeling. Creating our life through the extended neural network, brings in the highest alignment, and creates an evolution of our consciousness.

In using this extended neural network, we access the manifesting process of the divine plan.

It's simple and beautiful.

Visualizing and feeling into the desired end result, creates an outcome in our bodies and in the world around us. This is why, what we believe is so important.

Whatever we believe inside, we create outside.

As above, so below.
Inner, to Outer.

Our hearts are always beating, always sending out energy and information; always influencing the field, based on what we feel and believe. This is how we create.

This is why, making sure that our beliefs support our dreams, and our alignment, is so important.

Humanity lost consciousness around this.

Because of all of the toxins and stress, our capacity to visualize and focus, has been impaired. Our minds are worried and, many times, consumed by: what is wrong, what is scandalous, and what is trending; as opposed to, what we are choosing to create. In general, for so many of us, our hearts are broken; we are carrying around so much pain.

This is why, it's so important to do the inner work to heal yourself; and create the mastery to, once again, remember; you are a child of God, sovereign in your own life.

The work of restoring yourself, is the work of restoring your relationship with God.

The clearer your body, mind, and emotions; the clearer your life.

Take care of your heart. Love and appreciate it. Feed it good food and positive emotions. If you are facing any problems, that are reflective of longstanding patterns, face them honestly. Look at who and what you have chosen to include, in your life. Examine how they make you feel, and why they are in your life. Take time, every day, to experience what your heart is telling you.

Your heart is, on a moment to moment basis, creating your reality. Participate in this consciously; and experience yourself as the divine creator, that you were born to be.

****

IT IS THROUGH THE POWER OF MY HEART, THAT I MANIFEST MY DREAMS AND DESIRES. MY HEART IS MANIFESTING MY ALIGNMENT AND THE DIVINE PLAN OF MY LIFE.

****

Exercise #35

The following is an exercise, developed by Gregg Braden, that helps to promote a balance, between the mind and the heart. It is also based, in part, on the work of Josiah Brandt.

Take some quiet time where you won't be disturbed. Relax and take a few deep breaths. Place your fingers, or palm, on the area of your heart, in a relaxed and gentle way.

Continue to breathe deeply; and allow yourself to focus on the area, where you are touching your heart, right in the center of your chest.

Purposefully, slow your breath down; and allow yourself to feel centered. This sends the body a message, that you are safe. Take your time, in doing this; and really, let yourself experience how good it feels to be present with your heart, and breath.

Choose one of the following, or a combination of the following, 4 emotions to feel:

Care
Appreciation
Compassion
Gratitude

Once you are experiencing the emotion(s), imagine that you are experiencing your goals, and dreams.

Pretend, you are doing, and experiencing, the things on your list. Allow yourself to experience this state for as long as you'd like. When you are finished surrender it to God, and go into deep gratitude; that it is already available to you, in the present.

****
THE POWER OF YOUR DIVINE HEART: HEALS ALL THINGS, CHANGES ALL THINGS; AND CREATES UNLIMITED GOODNESS, IN YOUR LIFE.

CHAPTER 36
CREATING A DAILY ROUTINE

Creating a daily routine, to help you achieve greater alignment in your manifesting process, can be extremely helpful.

I have included a list below, with a few practices that work well together. You will know what works best for you.

Consistency is the key. One of the best times to do this is in the morning. It's important to maintain the spirit, of the practices, throughout the day. For example, if you choose to start the day with a gratitude list, continue to use gratitude throughout the day. By allowing yourself to integrate these practices, more and more each day, your time will be spent increasing higher frequencies. Alignment will automatically happen through the consistency of your efforts.

Pace yourself. Build slowly and surely so that you can maintain the momentum as opposed to doing too much too soon and becoming overwhelmed. This will allow you to have greater success in understanding and using the ideas. Follow your intuition about what would be a positive next step for you and what you may want to add to your routine. The right attitude and consistency is the key.

Some Suggestions For A Beginning Daily Routine

-Gratitude and Forgiveness
-Spending daily time with your manifesting list
-Intention and Intuition
-Unity Consciousness
-Showing Unconditional Love, Kindness, and Compassion

****

THROUGH CONSISTENCY AND DAILY EFFORT, DIVINE ALIGNMENT IN ALL THINGS IS POSSIBLE.

****

Exercise #36

Take some time and play around with the different ideas in this book to use in your daily routine. Come up with a few ideas to start with that you can commit to. Set a day and time to begin and then take action. Create a momentum and help yourself stay committed to your routine. Record your progress daily in your journal. List the different outcomes that happen as a result of the new activities that you've added to your life.

****

Every day you take guided action towards God, is a new day of allowing the divine plan to shine through your life. Enjoy the journey.

CHAPTER 37
MANIFESTING AT A GLANCE

YOU ARE A POWERFUL, DIVINE BEING CAPABLE OF CREATING VAST GOODNESS FOR YOURSELF AND OTHERS.

God has created a divine plan for your life which includes: happiness, joy, abundance, nurturing loving relationships, satisfying partnerships, a wonderful, fulfilling career, based on sharing your gifts; and a specific purpose that only you can fulfill.

The divine plan for your life is accessed, through the action of divine alignment.

Divine alignment is accessed through: setting your intention, using and following your intuition, staying surrendered, and keeping your frequency and vibration high.

God wants you to live the best life possible. Staying mindful of this, will support you in opening up to receive greater, and greater, gifts from the Divine. It will also help you maintain high levels of self-love, self-care, and self-esteem. Know the Divine is seeking to shower you with love, happiness, and abundance. Allow yourself to receive all of the goodness that God is bringing to you.

HOLD A CLEAR VISION

Get a clear vision of what you want to manifest, either through: a goal, a vision, or an internal understanding. Allow yourself to embrace the desires of your heart; and understand, your inspired dreams and visions, are part of a comprehensive divine plan, for the planet. Make a list of the dreams and desires of your heart. Go into as much detail as possible.

SPEND TIME WITH YOUR MANIFESTING LIST EVERYDAY

Spend time, on a daily basis, looking at the things on your list and creating the feelings of already having them. Use your imagination to make the experience as real as possible. If you feel any resistance while working with your list, process and transmute it.

INTEND

Set your intention daily to access divine alignment, to live the divine plan of your life, and to take whatever inspired action you are guided to take. Using the power of your intention will help you in your creative process and in staying connected to God's energy.

USE YOUR GIFTS

Seek and find your gifts. Be determined to use and enjoy them. God gives you your gifts and works through them, to create the divine plan, and to help others. We have been conditioned to think, we can't be abundant through using our gifts. THIS IS NOT TRUE. We are abundantly provided for, when we use our gifts. They create more joy, more fun, and more alignment, in our lives. This helps everyone, and raises the frequency of the planet.

INTUITION AND INSPIRED ACTION

Clarifying and following your intuition, creates greater alignment. It allows you to access the divine plan. When we, initially, start to work with our intuition, we may not get it quite right. This is because, we may be receiving information from our egos, or our subconscious programming, etc. When we clarify our guidance, we open the flood gates to divine information. Take consistent steps in following the guidance that you get. Taking inspired action, and following your intuition, causes it to grow stronger. Ignoring your intuition, causes it slow down, and come to you less frequently.

MAINTAIN GRATITUDE AND POSITIVE ENERGY

The type of energy you hold within your body, thoughts, and feelings affects your life; your capacity to maintain alignment, and the nature of your manifestations. Staying positive, compassionate, and kind keeps your frequency high, and helps other people. Make a daily gratitude list, and carry the energy of gratitude throughout the day. Count all of your blessings, and notice all of the things, in your life, that are going well.

LOVE AND HONOR YOURSELF

Remember that you are holy and divine. Participate in joyous and loving activities, that allow you to feel respected and honored. Radiate unconditional love for yourself, and for all in a surrendered state. In doing this, you will begin to actively engage the source of abundance, that lives within you, and only wants your highest good.

MONITOR YOUR BELIEFS / PROCESS ANY BLOCKS

You create according to your beliefs. Whatever you believe you can have, you will allow yourself to receive. Monitor your beliefs. They may or may not be true. If you run into any unconscious blocks, or you find you were able to create at a great pace; and then suddenly you weren't able to move forward, take time out. Be present with the block or situation. Ask God, or your higher self, for the insight needed to transmute and heal the blocks. Feel what comes up. Process it and then surrender it to God.

<u>Trust and have deep faith, that you will receive whatever is in the highest and best for you.</u>

EXPANSIVE THINKING AND IMAGINATION

The more expanded your thinking, the more positive energy you allow into your being and world. Your imagination is deeply linked to your soul and subconscious. Use it wisely to send messages, about what you would like to experience, to these parts of yourself. Visualize and daydream; and again, make sure you believe you can have it. Remember, God has created all of the experiences of the divine plan in the now. It's all already available.

PURPOSE

It's important to understand, why you want to manifest the different goals on your list. If you are seeking to manifest a new house, become clear about why. What purpose will it serve in your life? How will it bring you more into divine alignment? The clearer you get about the importance of your goal, the easier and faster the manifestation will happen.

UNITY CONSCIOUSNESS

Maintain unity consciousness. Remembering that you are of God; and that, God lives within you is the great goal of life. Seeing the divine energy in all people, places, and things; and remembering that nothing is separate from this energy, will support you in keeping your frequency high, and your alignment strong. Maintaining unity consciousness, will bring your dreams to you in ease and grace. It will change your consciousness and the world. We are a collective, and we are all one.

CLEAR YOUR LIFE OF NEGATIVITY

Take steps to heal; and release any negative emotions, negative situations, negative people, and negative influences that may be in your life. As you work to transform the negativity in your world, you will find the frequency of your life rises; and you will experience more joy and fulfillment. Your life will continue to get better and better.

SURRENDER AND FORGIVENESS

Surrender all of your goals to God, "this or better." Surrender all of your experiences, and any negativity you are experiencing, to God. If you are having problems, surrender them to God; and completely let them go. Allow people to have their own journey. Refuse to hold yourself back. Through forgiveness and surrender, you can move through any negative situation. You can heal the deepest wounds, and you can bring peace and prosperity into your world. When we forgive unconditionally, and release all blame, guilt, resentment, etc., we are free; and we gain an important education and healing.

RAISE YOUR FREQUENCY ON A DAILY, CONSISTENT BASIS

Choose to flood your body and life, with love and joy. Acknowledge the Divine in all you do. Choose activities that raise your frequency, and help to keep it high.

OFFER YOUR BEST / BE OPEN TO RECEIVE

Remember that manifesting is a circuit. It starts with what we give out to the world, and it is completed through what we allow ourselves to receive. Offer the world your best. Open yourself to receiving all of the goodness, happiness and abundance God has for you.

UNCONDITIONAL LOVE, KINDNESS AND COMPASSION

You are constantly manifesting through the energy of your heart. Intentionally hold the highest feelings and positive thoughts. This creates the extended neural network, where the heart and mind work together. Further activate the divine matrix within yourself. Cultivate continuous states of unconditional love, kindness and compassion. Bathe in them. Breathe them in, and shower your life with them.

USE YOUR TOOLS & PROCESSES CONSISTENTLY / DAILY

The more you use the tools in this book, the better your life will get; and the more you will achieve and stay in divine alignment.

PART III

SACRED PRAYERS, PROCESSES AND TOOLS

CHAPTER 38
THE SACRED PROCESSES AND TOOLS

Divine alignment is a lifestyle. It's a journey that reveals itself; day by day, building in intensity and beauty as we surrender to it, and enjoy our relationship with God.

In the chapters that follow, you will find a collection of the sacred processes, and tools I use to maintain my own alignment, and that I share with my clients. I have included many different kinds of tools, and I suggest that they be used with regularity and consistency. They will help keep your frequency high, and your alignment strong. Becoming familiar with them, and using them on a regular basis, will allow you to engage an energetic component; that will help you move forward in greater ease, and integrate new changes successfully. They will expand your consciousness and increase your personal power; supporting you in your journey to create an abundant life, through accessing the divine plan.

CHAPTER 39
INTRODUCTION TO THE SACRED PRAYERS / MAPS OF INTENT

The following section, contains the sacred prayers or "maps of intent"; that I use daily in every aspect of my life and work. These prayers were gifted to me from God and the divine realm. They are extremely powerful and effective, and can be used constantly throughout the day, without fear of overuse. The clearer we are, the more balance we create in our lives, and the stronger the alignment.

I have created a wide variety of prayers for all kinds of uses, from clearing the subconscious, to clearing items and environmental toxins. For the purpose of this book, however, I have chosen to only include the prayers directly related to divine alignment, manifestation, and personal empowerment.

There is a comprehensive collection of the sacred prayers on our website. Many can also be found on the prayer app, which has a special format to allow the prayers to be played, automatically, throughout the day. Because I am saying the prayers, on the app, there is the added benefit of receiving my energetic support while listening.

If you want to use the prayers to help others, who are not present, simply say the prayer or play it, from the app; and intend it be used for the person you are seeking to help.

CHAPTER 40
THE SACRED PRAYERS / MAPS OF INTENT

Below are the sacred prayers, or maps of intent. I encourage people to speak them with authority. God truly appreciates a bit of feistiness. As mentioned earlier, use them as often as you feel led. They cannot be overused; each time you use them, they create a clearing and a healing.

PRAYER OF PROTECTION

I am of God.
I ground myself to the Earth.

I command you, God, to place a bubble of unconditional love, from the ultimate dimension, around me; to protect me from any negative entities, any fractals thereof, manipulations, and any transmissional frequencies, that are not for my highest good, through all space/time continuum, in every dimension.

I thank you God, and send you my unconditional love.
So Be It / Amen

PYRAMID PRAYER OF PROTECTION

I am of God.

I ground myself to the Earth.

I command you, God, to create an Esoteric Pyramid around me, with me in the king's chamber, on the Holy Grail, and the Arc of the Covenant. I program this pyramid with the blueprint of my DNA, and the keys of Enoch; so as, not to allow anything except for my highest good to enter, through all space/time continuum in any dimension.

Dear God, I command that you align it now and track the alignment, with the changes in the Earth's polarity and activate it now.

I thank you God, and I send you my unconditional love.
So Be It / Amen

THE 12 ESOTERIC MERKABA FIELD PRAYER OF PROTECTION

I am of God.

I ground myself to the Earth.

I command you, God, to create 12 Esoteric Merkaba fields around me; to protect me from any negative entities, fractals thereof, manipulations, and transmissional frequencies that are not for my highest good.

Optimize the vibration of these Merkaba fields.

Program these Merkaba fields with the blueprint of my DNA, and the keys of Enoch; so as, not to allow anything to enter, except for my highest good, through all space/time continuum in every dimension.

I thank you, God, and send you my unconditional love.

So Be It / Amen

PRAYER TO DISABLE RADIONIC MACHINES FROM YOUR LIFE

I am of God.

I ground myself to the Earth.

I command you, God, to disable all the radionic machines that are affecting my life now. Disable all of the factories they were created in.

I bring all the beings involved, no matter how remote, before you God, for justice in only the way you know how. It's not for us to judge them. Therefore, we release them to you with unconditional love and forgiveness.

I thank you, God, and send you my unconditional love.
So Be It / Amen

PRAYER TO REMOVE SPIRITUAL ATTACK

I am of God.

I ground myself to the Earth.

I command you, God, to remove all the negative remote viewers, remove all manipulations, and transmissional frequencies, that are not for my highest good, through all space/time continuum in every dimension.

Remove all the machines and redundancies creating all these frequencies, infinite levels high and infinite levels wide, in every dimension.

I bring all the beings before you, God, for justice in only the way you know how. I release them to you with unconditional love and forgiveness.

I thank you, God, and send you my unconditional love.
So Be It / Amen

PRAYER TO REMOVE HOLOGRAPHIC INSERTS

I am of God.

I ground myself to the Earth.

I command you, God, to remove this holographic insert from my current space/time continuum in this dimension. I bring all the beings, who created it, before you God, for justice in only the way you know how. I release them all to you, God, with unconditional love and forgiveness.

I thank you, God, and send you my unconditional love.
So Be It / Amen

PRAYER TO REMOVE MANIPULATION FROM YOUR PERSONAL LIFE

I am of God.
I ground myself to the Earth.

I command you, God, to break all spells, curses, and ancient rituals in my life that are not good and true. I command you to remove all negative remote viewers. Remove all radionics machines affecting my life now.

I command you, to rebalance any manipulation of the space/time continuum, in this 3rd dimensional world, and through all space/time continuum, in every dimension.

I bring all the beings involved, with any of my personal manipulation infinite levels high and infinite levels wide, through all space/time continuum, in every dimension, before you God, for justice in only the way you know how. It's not for us to judge them, therefore, we release them to you, God, with unconditional love and forgiveness.

I thank you, God, and send you my unconditional love.
So Be It / Amen

PRAYER TO REMOVE CONSCIOUS AND SUBCONSCIOUS BLOCKS AND 3RD DIMENSIONAL CONDITIONING

I am of God.
I ground myself to the Earth.

I command you, God, to remove, from my being, all conscious and subconscious blocks, and 3rd dimensional conditioning, infinite levels high and infinite levels wide, through all space/time continuum, in every dimension.

I command you, God, to flood all these timelines, through all space/time continuum, with your Divine Love.

I thank you, God, and I send you my unconditional love.
So Be It / Amen

PRAYER TO REMOVE LOW VIBRATIONAL PARTICLES AND DISABLE PARTICLE ACCELERATORS FROM YOUR LIFE

I am of God.
I ground myself to the Earth.

I command you, God, to remove all low vibrational particles, from my body, and disable all on and off planet particle accelerators involved, through all space/time continuum, in every dimension. Close all interdimensional portals, and rebalance the equilibrium of the time/space continuum, in every dimension.

I bring all the beings involved in creating this manipulation, infinite levels wide and infinite levels high, before you, God, for justice in only the way you know how. It's not for us to judge them, therefore, we release them to you, with unconditional love and forgiveness.

I thank you God and send you my unconditional love.
So Be It / Amen

PRAYER TO REMOVE AN ENTITY FROM A PERSON'S BODY

THIS PRAYER MUST BE SAID WITH ABSOLUTE POWER, CONVICTION AND AUTHORITY FOR THE PRAYER TO ACTIVATE.

I am of God.

I ground myself to the Earth.

I command the Melchizedek Beings, to open a portal from the Ultimate Dimension around the person this prayer is for, and close it off underneath them. I command the Melchizedek Beings, to escort all the negative entities and fractals thereof out, of their body, now. I bless and forgive them for their manipulation, and release them to the Ultimate Dimension, with unconditional love and forgiveness.

I command that they place 12 Esoteric Merkaba Fields around the person this prayer is for, with their sacral point in the center of the Merkaba Fields; to protect them from any negative entities, fractals thereof, manipulations, and transmissional frequencies, that are not for their highest good, through all space/time continuum, in every dimension.

I thank you, God, and send you my unconditional love.
So Be It / Amen

FOOD BLESSING AND REVIBRATION PRAYER

I am of God.
I ground myself to the Earth.

I command you, God, to correct and rebalance any modifications made to this food that are not of God; optimize the nutritional value and remove all the toxins. Bless the souls of all the plants and animals, that have given their lives to provide my body nutrition.

I thank you, God, and I send you my unconditional love.
So Be It / Amen

PRAYER TO REVIBRATE PERSONAL DRINKING WATER

I am of God.
I ground myself to the Earth.

I command you, God, to remove all negative entities from this water; optimize its vibration; and program it with the blueprint of its crystalline structure.

I thank you, God, and I send you my unconditional love.
So Be It / Amen

PRAYER TO REMOVE CONTAMINANTS AND REBALANCE EARTH'S PLANETARY WATER SYSTEM

I am of God.

I ground myself to the Earth.

I command you, God, to assist in the opening of a portal, from the Ultimate Dimension, to transmute the biomolecular crystalline structure of the entire planetary water system and its elementals; to release all the toxins and negative entities, energies, and fractals thereof, that are not for the highest good of humanity and all beings.

I command you, God, to reactivate the cellular memory blueprint of the water, and program it with Divine Love and the Sacred Keys of Enoch; so as, not to allow anything except for the highest good, of all beings on the planet, to enter and affect the planetary water system.

I thank you, God, and I send you my unconditional love.

So Be It / Amen

PRAYER TO NEUTRALIZE AND REMOVE CHEMTRAILS

I am of God.

I ground myself to the Earth.

I command you, God, to neutralize and remove all the negative and harmful substances contained in the chemtrails above.

I command that you alter the biological and molecular structure, through all space/time continuum, in every dimension; to convert these trails into harmless water vapor; so as, to protect all the humans, animals, and plants that inhabit our 3rd dimensional universe.

I thank you, God, and I send you my unconditional love.
So Be It / Amen

PRAYER TO BLOCK OUT LUCIFERIAN SPIRITS AND FREQUENCIES FROM MULTIMEDIA

I am of God.
I ground myself to the Earth.

I command you, God, to remove all the luciferian spirits and vibration from this multimedia. I bring all the beings involved with the manipulation; infinite levels high, infinite levels wide, no matter how remote; before you, God, for justice in only the way you know how. I release them all to you, God, with unconditional love and forgiveness.

I thank you, God, and send you my unconditional love.
So Be It / Amen

PRAYER TO REMOVE RADIONIC MANIPULATION FROM COMPUTER AND ELECTRONIC EQUIPMENT

I am of God.

I ground myself to the Earth.

I command you, God, to remove all the radionic manipulations, from this computer and electronic equipment, that is not for my highest good, through all space time/continuum, in every dimension. I bring all the beings involved with this manipulation, no matter how remote, in every dimension before you, God, for justice in only the way you know how. I release them to you with unconditional love and forgiveness.

I thank you, God, and send you my unconditional love.
So Be It / Amen

PRAYER TO CLEAR AND REPROGRAM CRYSTALS

I am of God.
I ground myself to the Earth.

I command you, God, to remove any negative energies or negative entities from this crystal. Optimize its vibration and program it with the blueprint, of my DNA and the keys of Enoch; so as, not to let anything, except for my highest good, to enter.

I thank you, God, and I send you my unconditional love.
So Be It / Amen

GROUNDING PRAYER

I am of God.
I ground myself to the Earth.

I accept this healing for my highest good.

I thank you, God, and I send you my unconditional love.
So Be It / Amen

LIFE PURPOSE PRAYER

I am of God.
I ground myself to the Earth.

I command you, God, to give me direction as to my highest life purpose; and to help me fulfil this purpose swiftly, effectively, and for the good of all concerned.

I command you to infuse me with the energy, strength, and inspiration needed to fulfill this job.

I thank you, God, and send you my unconditional love.
So Be It / Amen

PRAYER TO RELEASE ANY CELLULAR MEMORY OR ESOTERIC TRANSFERENCE FROM PAST LIFE

(Sat 3x or 9x to activate the power within the SACRED NUMBERS.)

I am of God.
I ground myself to the Earth.

I come before you, God, for forgiveness, for anything I have done in any past life, to infinitum, through all space and time, in any dimension; that has been brought back into this lifetime, and is affecting my life now.

I release it all to you, God, with unconditional love;

I thank you, God, and send you my unconditional love.
So Be It / Amen

PRAYER TO RELEASE PAST LIFE CONNECTION ISSUES

(Say 3x or 9x to activate the power within the SACRED NUMBERS.)

I am of God.

I ground myself to the Earth.

I come before you, God, for forgiveness, for anything I have done in any past life, to infinitum, though all space/time, in any dimension; that has been brought back into this lifetime, and is affecting my relationship with this person now.

I release it all to you, God, with unconditional love;

I thank you, God, and send you my unconditional love.

So Be It / Amen

PRAYER TO FACILITATE A LOVED ONE'S SOUL WHO HAS PASSED ON TO THE GOD REALM

I am of God.
I ground myself to the Earth.

I command you, God, to open a portal over my loved one, for whom this prayer is for.

I thank you, loved one, for whom this prayer is for; for being in the classroom, and on your spiritual journey, on this timeline, in this lifetime, in this 3rd Dimensional world. I love, honor, and bless you for all of your creations in this lifetime.

I command the creator gods to escort my loved one's soul, back to the 5th Dimensional world, to proceed on their spiritual journey.

I thank you, God, and I send you my unconditional love.
So Be It / Amen

CHAPTER 41
MEDITATION

Meditation is one of the most important tools that we have. It helps us to maintain our connection to God, to receive higher levels of Source energy; and to remain focused, calm, centered, and aware.

So much of what people experience today, is the result of feeling stressed and disconnected. We end up on a hamster wheel of never ending "to-do" lists, "over the top" multi-tasking, too many "screens" open at once, video gaming, social media, toxins, microwaves, stressful home life, etc.

Being busy and worn down is our "new normal". So many people are experiencing increasingly high levels of depression, anxiety, stress, and scatteredness. All of these states are debilitating.

When we meditate, we temporarily suspend all of the chatter in our minds. We plug into our own inner divinity. We allow for the stillness that is our source to flood through us and we get a chance to rest within the peace. This divine stillness, is the balm that our souls need. The universal life force energy builds, within us, when we meditate: restoring, rejuvenating, and rebalancing; our mind, body, emotions, soul, and spirit.

People, sometimes initially, have difficulty learning how to relax themselves in order to meditate. You may have to make an effort to clear your mind, so that you can be still. With persistence, you will be able to master the process.

As you meditate, you will begin to experience a positive change within yourself. You will embody more of who you are through embodying higher, and higher, frequencies. Life begins to take on a new quality, reflective of the divine meditative energy you are holding and experiencing. You will access and carry around more peace, equanimity, serenity, and joy. This will, in turn, help you to create more happiness, success and alignment. Those who meditate daily, find that their lives are more enjoyable, more meaningful, more balanced, more successful, and more peaceful.

There are many forms of meditation offered online; from guided meditations, to simple methods, such as, being present with your breath, or focusing your awareness on a particular point. Considering the importance of thought within our lives; it only makes sense to make every effort to gain the greatest mental stability and emotional composure. Make the effort to find a meditative practice that resonates with you. Even if you can only devote 5 to 10 minutes a day, stick with it. It will make a huge difference in your life, and in your alignment.

As mentioned before, we also have a meditation app that features a variety of different kinds of meditations. Our meditations have the added benefit of being energetically supported, so that you receive additional help from the angelic realm and the Divine.

CHAPTER 42
THE CHAKRAS /
CHAKRA MEDITATION

As mentioned before, our entire physiology, (ie., mind, body, spirit, soul, emotion, etheric body, etc.) is designed to help us maintain divine alignment. The chakra system is central, in all of this. The chakras are energy vortexes, within the body, that receive energy from your inner divine; and circulate the energy throughout the entire body. They take in energy, and they release energy. When they are working correctly, all aspects of life balance out and self-correct.

The energy of each chakra corresponds to a particular physical and emotional function. In the past, it's been known that humans have seven primary chakras. Now, with the awakening of humanity, and the planetary ascension; new primary chakras have opened, within our etheric system, increasing the number to 13. These new primary chakras act as a gateway, between dimensions, helping us to adjust and respond to the new frequencies, as they gently open.

THE ORIGIONAL CHAKRAS:

Root Chakra

The root or base chakra anchors you to the earth, providing solidity and grounding. It gives you a sense of who you are. When balanced and functioning properly, this chakra provides courage and self-confidence. When out of alignment, one can easily descend into a state of lack, fear, and victimhood; and become consumed with the struggle to survive. To release your innate stores of courage and sense of self, take a deep breath, feel your connection to the earth, and your wholeness.

Sacral Chakra

The sacral or sex chakra, is your emotional energy center. This is where sexual desire and animal instinct comes from. When balanced, your creativity flows and you are able to feel joy. When out of balance: problems, addictions, and perversions can arise; including, emotional instability, and the inability to separate pain from pleasure. Balancing this chakra will help lay claim to your emotions and your self-confidence. It will help you to experience true intimacy, with a loving partner; and it will enable you to experience true joy, without limitation.

Solar Plexus Chakra

The solar plexus chakra is located just above the naval, and is known as your power center. Here is where will, confidence, and your true power reside. When in alignment; discernment, wisdom, self-control, and common sense clarify. Your strength comes from within, and you no longer depend on others for their approval. Here is where you manifest your highest desires. When out of alignment, your light source is cut off, and you feed off of the energy of others.

Heart Chakra

Unconditional Love, hope, and faith emanate from the heart chakra; which serves as a doorway to your higher dimensions. When unbalanced, you react from a primal, instinctual level; as governed by the lower chakras. In this state you experience hurt in an extreme way. You may lash out when feeling wounded, jealous, or in pain. When in balance, your heart chakra connects you to your higher chakras; and allows compassion, love and empathy to flow. You can freely love the universe, the creator; and trust in your divinity. Jealousy, spite, and fear disappear; as an open heart chakra enables you to unite with all creatures.

Throat Chakra

The throat chakra governs the frequency and vibrations, of our thoughts and words. Our reality is created by what we think and say. It's not just the words we use, but the energy they contain that connects us with our highest state of being. When the throat chakra is out of balance, our words project fearful, negative, reactionary thoughts. To move further into divine alignment, your thoughts and words must be mastered. Balancing the throat chakra will help you use language that projects your inner light and truth; magnifying your ability to communicate in all ways; along with, magnifying your positive intention for the future.

Third Eye Chakra

Your third eye is the energy center of your highest psychic sense; where, intuition beyond discernment flourishes, as well as, your innate wisdom. When the third eye is cleared and opened, you will see with clarity; and know things innately, without input from others. The third eye opens the connection between you and your higher self, and allows you to commune with spirit. New ideas, information, and modes of creativity become available to you. An open third eye leads to the blossoming of our highest consciousness. When the third eye is open, your ascension is underway.

Crown Chakra

The crown chakra is the culmination of the energy centers located below it. When open, the crown chakra signifies the flowering of your divine self, preparing you for your connection with the God Realm. Here, comes full understanding and connection, as you reach for God consciousness and unity with others. As you live and radiate love, light, and divine truth you will be infused with God consciousness.

THE NEW CHAKRAS

The new chakras are a part of our growing crystalline light body, harmonizing and expanding our energies; as we move forward, as a planet, into a greater awakening...and into the 5th dimension.

Diaphragm Chakra

This chakra is the gateway to the fulfillment of your soul purpose. Our self-imposed restrictions are stored here, as well as, our contradictory life experiences. Breathe deeply, filling your diaphragm. This will help you to work through these temporary restraints. Breathing deeply, will help to purge them so self-empowerment can occur. This is an unfolding process which happens on its own as you step into, greater and greater, alignment and awaken.

Thymus Chakra

The thymus, or second heart chakra, is your bridge to unconditional love. While the heart chakra is more in tune with love between individuals; the thymus, or second heart, increases your unconditional love for everything. It increases your loving connection to the Divine.

Well of Dreams Chakra

Located at the base of the head directly above the neck, this is a communication center that receives, and regulates, the flow of messages from Source. Keeping this chakra functioning properly will help you achieve universal consciousness.

Pituitary

Located near the pineal in the center of your head, the pituitary chakra interacts with the other chakras, as well as, the body's glandular and hormonal systems, harmonizing conflicting energies and regulating interdimensional energies.

Universal Female

Situated above the head to the left, the universal female chakra controls empathy, creativity, non-linear thinking, intuition, and motherly love.

Universal Male

The universal male chakra, found above the head to the right, regulates your practical perceptions of reality, analytical precepts, protective instincts, and your ability to follow through on complicated tasks.

****

Take time, and sit quietly, where you won't be disturbed. Breathe deeply. Say and feel this completely, "I am now accessing and integrating: the power of unity, oneness, and my connection with the Earth, and all abundance." Breathe deeply.

Spin the sphere of light, representing your base chakra, until it spins so quickly and it bursts open with sparks of shimmering light.

Envision the energy and light rising from the first chakra, to the second.

Breathe deeply. Say and feel this completely; "I am one with the Divine Creator Source."

By opening the base chakra, you are activating the Creator's light and causing the energy to move upward in a column of white light. This is, an energy, usually known as the *kundalini*. This is a Sanskrit term for the coiled energy, located at the base of the spine. When released, this energy travels up the spine, energizing each chakra; until reaching the universal "male/female" chakra, located over the crown, exploding in a state of bliss, and opening your connection, to the Creator Gods.

If your chakras are blocked, to the point where you feel stuck, you may want to seek help in getting them cleared. The Melchizedek beings and other angelic beings I work with, help suck out the negative energies within each chakra point and prevent these energies from going into the glands and organs, which can make you sick. Opening the chakras, and aligning them this way, greatly helps in the attainment of divine alignment, the expansion of consciousness, and in healing sickness.

CHAKRA MEDITATION AND VISUALIZATION

Breathe in God's light, while superimposing the infinity sign over each sphere/chakra, to accelerate the release of ingrained, stagnant energy, and patterns.

Imagine, as you breathe energy into each chakra, that an energy vortex opens.

Project the perfect vibration of that chakra, upward, into the next chakra while saying, upward on the line:

1. Base Chakra: *"I have all I need. I am strong and secure."*
2. Second Chakra: *"I am creative, stable, and intimate in the right times."*
3. Third Chakra/Diaphragm: *"I am fulfilling my life purpose."*

4. Fourth/Solar Plexus: *"I am vital with an inner personal power."*
5. Fifth/Heart Chakra: *"I unconditionally love all, and all love me."*
6. Sixth/Thymus Chakra: *"I unconditionally love the Divine Creator, Mother Earth, and all the Earth's inhabitants."*
7. Seventh/Throat Chakra: *"My thoughts and words express my highest goals."*
8. Eighth/Well of Dreams Chakra: *"I welcome all messages from the highest God source."*
9. Ninth/Pituitary Chakra: *"I harmonize with all energies, within and without, as long as they are in keeping with the energy of the Divine Creator."*
10. Tenth/Third Eye Chakra: *"I see all and know all. I connect to my highest self."*
11. Eleventh/Crown Chakra: *"I know myself and God, the Creator. I ascend to the highest realm."*
12. Universal Female Chakra: *"I allow my female energies to flow smoothly."*
13. Universal Male Chakra: *"I allow my male energies to flow smoothly."*

As the creator light, is released from each chakra, it flows upward, repeating in each chakra until reaching the crown.

Take time to do this exercise regularly. Consistency will provide great results.

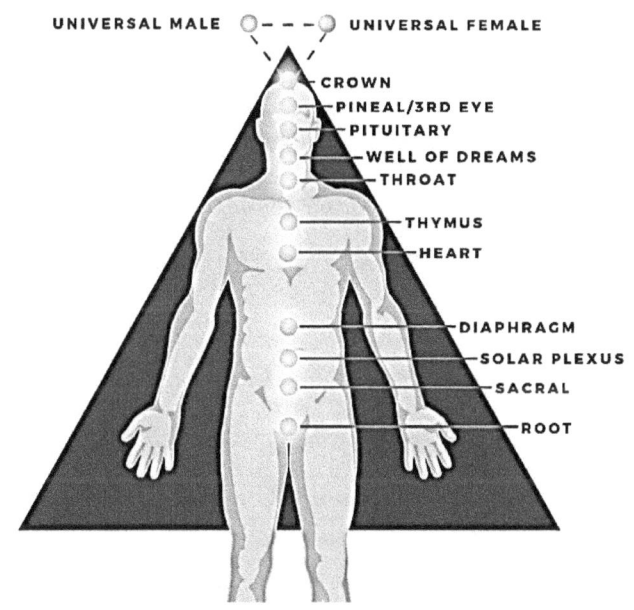

CHAPTER 43
WISDOM BEYOND FORGIVENESS

"Wisdom Beyond Forgiveness", is an energetic process to help heal and resolve past issues. It clears and rebalances painful experiences; creating wholeness and greater alignment. It allows you to grow stronger from these experiences, as opposed to, sustaining the traumas. Information and wisdom is gained, and we are able to walk away from situations with the gifts.

Using it, in connection, to any disappointing, abusive, or upsetting situations will help release the energy from the situation or incident. This, in turn, will bring a healing to all involved, and help clear your consciousness. The clearer your consciousness, the faster and more profound your manifestations.

Maybe an individual had a parent who yelled at them, and made them feel insignificant when they were young. Once the person grows up, they may have difficulty forming healthy relationships; because they feel inadequate, or maybe they are afraid to stand up for themselves, in business situations; because they are afraid of being targeted by others. Many times, traditional psychotherapy is unable to create truly lasting, significant healing. "Forgive and move on with your life." is among the advice often given.

We need something more, in order to move beyond the traumas and pain in our lives. We need something that will create an inner shift. In order to overcome obstacles, make positive progress in life, and continue to evolve, more and more, into our divine selves; we must develop *"Wisdom Beyond Forgiveness"*.

Growing beyond forgiveness into wisdom is a crucial step in our evolution, at this point in time. It is important to bless all of those who have: wronged, hurt, or harmed us; or our loved ones, in any way. It's important to release those who have violated us, and allow them their journey. This may be harder to do than it seems. We can easily tell how much wounding we have sustained, by how difficult this is to do. If you find it nearly impossible to do, then you are holding on to immense wounding and pain. You have to keep revisiting the pain, no matter how much it hurts, until you release it. If you don't go through the process of being with and releasing, the energy and emotions around the event, you may spend your whole life being a victim of that wrongdoing.

When we take time to process and heal the emotions, within us, we take responsibility for our own healing.

When moving into wisdom, you grow through forgiveness into understanding. If, for example, you have an abusive father who continuously calls you a despicable name; realize that he is on his own journey. He must come to terms with his behavior and change, if he is to evolve. It is not for you to do this for him. In the same respect, it's not ok that you were mistreated. You must move forward creating healing and safety for yourself, while respecting him and all involved. As you do, recognize, that because this happened; you can change the way you view things. You can see this as a blessing, because his journey has helped you become the person you are today. Even though there was a tremendous amount of pain involved, the experience educated you. It brought you strength and understanding.

Obstacles and difficulties always bring an education. Embrace the growth they bring, and you will achieve wisdom beyond forgiveness.

But how do we do this?

Take some time in a quiet place, where you will not be disturbed.

Begin, by holding the memory of a painful situation, that occurred, in your past. Maybe it's more than mild abuse. Maybe it is a terrible trauma like murder or rape.

Release the incident by saying, "I release you,". Then, in your mind's eye, say to the transgressor, "Bless you for this journey."

Thank them for the blessing of participating in your life's journey and your growth. Then bless them for their journey, and flood them with unconditional love. You don't have to work to forgive them; because they've helped you become the person you are today, which is much stronger, capable, and resilient.

Get their face in your mind and say:

I thank you for participating in my journey.
I bless you on your journey.
And, I send you my Unconditional Love.

Then flood them with Unconditional Love from your heart chakra.

They are on their life path with all the karma that is associated with it. Both of you, are in a 3D classroom and here to learn. Both of you, have grown spiritually by the incident. Both of you, have the power to understand the impact. And now, you have allowed the person involved to continue on his or her journey, regardless of whether or not they grow.

It's important not to judge their journey. That's not for us to get involved in. It's up to the Divine, and up to them to take care of the karma, they've created. If they don't ask for forgiveness in this lifetime, they'll review their life when they pass on. When they go before God, they will revisit all of the situations they've been involved in while experiencing the hurt and trauma, they created. Forgiveness will be given at that point, and karma will be reset.

Why not just forgive them and move on?

The incident, or series of incidents, has caused you to grow. There is no need to forgive when the experience has been, in its own way, a blessing. The transgressor, undoubtedly, did not have this in mind when hurting you; and that's where forgiveness comes in. True enlightenment comes from expressing gratitude for the blessing, of the growth, the situation has provided you. This is true forgiveness. Just talking about it doesn't work. You have to move, through the forgiveness, into wisdom and unconditional love. The idea of wisdom beyond forgiveness may provoke strong emotions; and perhaps, even outrage, from those who do not understand it.

But, growing beyond forgiveness, into gratitude, is to achieve what so few fail to obtain: Divine Wisdom.

Here is a healing affirmation that is extremely powerful. When you find yourself in a situation that is difficult to bless, the person, who has inflicted harm on you or your loved ones, say the following:

I move beyond forgiveness to understanding.
I have compassion, kindness and unconditional love for all.

It bears mentioning again, that understanding and forgiving the person or situation is not enough. Wisdom is a far more powerful state, than just forgiveness. You achieve it by blessing the situation and the individual. Holding gratitude in your heart does not make you a victim. Instead, it empowers you and vastly improves all aspects of your life.

GOING UP THE CHANNEL

Here, is another important energetic process to help heal and change the past. I call it, *"Going Up The Channel And Altering The Past Timeline"*. This is going back in time and injecting unconditional love, into a "past situation". This completely alters the timeline. Doing this, moves the unconditional love vibration up the timeline to the present time. It changes the paradigm of that situation, including all the dynamics between individuals.

When you are ready to do this, again, take some time; and make sure you will be undisturbed.

Start by visualizing the situation. For example, suppose you're in the midst of a massive argument with someone…send this individual unconditional love in a strong blast.

Say to them:

I thank you for the journey.
I am blessed for the journey, and I thank you for your participation in my journey.
I bless you on your journey.
And, I send you my unconditional love.

Remember to feel that unconditional love flowing into them from your heart chakra.

For other past experiences, you can also try this:

Visualize the past trauma or abuse, verbal, emotional or physical. Hold that situation in your mind and walk through what happened.

When you have finished reviewing the incident look at the person and say:

I thank you for participating in my journey and for allowing me to spiritually grow.
I forgive you.
I bless you on your journey.
I send you unconditional love.

You have to *feel* the unconditional love coming out of your heart. Do not just say it.

Repeat: *I am blessed for the journey, and I am blessed by unconditional love.*

Again, you must feel that love coming from your heart chakra. This is the same with all spiritual things, whether you are engaged with affirmations, meditation, or anything else. Don't just say it. Feel it. Be it.

Doing this changes the former energy of that timeline. The unconditional love will go up the timeline to change the dynamic, of that paradigm, and affect what is happening now. Another way of explaining this, is that firing unconditional love into the past; will change, not only the past, but also, the current dynamic for everyone. It will even change the nature of your relationship with the people involved.

Watch what happens if you silently say to people, who have harmed you, "I forgive you unconditionally."

From that moment on they will react to you in a very different way.

ALTERING YOUR SPACE / TIME CONTINUUM

In order to truly change the space/time continuum, alter the effects of the past; and work to heal timelines; focus as you say, "I forgive you."

Focus on the impact of your life's journey while sending all involved unconditional love. Really feel it as you send love out to them. Feel the unconditional love vibration being injected into the timeline. Focus on the positive impact of that situation on your journey. Everything has a positive impact, even the worst sort of experiences. Using unconditional love in this way will change all of the dynamics. It creates the deepest healings, on every level, for everyone involved.

Unconditional love will ultimately save us all.

CHAPTER 44
AKASHIC RECORD CLEARING AND MEDITATION

The Akashic records, are an energetic database that contain all information relating to every human soul in existence. They store the information about what every individual has ever thought, felt, said, and done; through all lifetimes, and in all dimensions. The Akashic records can't be tampered with; but if there has been any tampering in your life, that has been recorded in your records, this tampering can be addressed and cleared.

One of the ways negative energies violate and manipulate people, is through blocking them from accessing the divine timeline. This causes people to be so frustrated, they go off on another timeline. In some cases, they may not ever reach the divine timeline while in a particular incarnation.

You can always heal and rebalance this, through your own awareness and efforts.

I have created an Akashic records clearing meditation, to remove and clear any blocks from the records, so that you can have greater ease in accessing your divine timeline. Once the blocks have been cleared, the energy around your life and the experiences you attract will take an amplified lift; as long as, you do the work to stay in alignment.

Becoming familiar with the Akashic records, and how they function, will allow you to have another powerful tool for creating change in your life. Because these records have been in place since the birth of your soul, they hold key information about you that can help you understand more about yourself; and how to create greater progress, and healing in your life.

For instance, someone may have had a lifetime where they had a lot of money; but unfortunately, were targeted, robbed, and attacked. If the trauma from that life time wasn't healed, most likely, they formed a belief system from that experience; that money is not safe, and if they do have it, they become a target. In this lifetime, they most likely, will have money issues; because they have beliefs that create resistance around having and using money. All of this information would be recorded in the Akashic Records, where the individual can learn about what happened to them, that created this trauma and belief. Once they access the records, and understand why and how, the beliefs and blocks formed; the healing often happens in a spontaneous way.

Sometimes, just having the information in the conscious mind is enough. From there, you can do whatever you are led to do to heal the trauma; so that, you can move forward in a healthy, balanced way. Having the needed information, from the Akashic records, saves a lot of time and energy.

In some ways, clearing the Akashic records is akin to clearing the biofield. The information in these databases is directly influencing our lives. When we can take greater responsibility for healing and rebalancing our past experiences; we find that, we have the ability to create more progress in our lives.

If you feel you have been blocked, you can always ask God for help in clearing and rebalancing any negativity, within the Akashic records. Send unconditional love up the timelines to release any blocks, which were put into place to throw you off course. You can seek help from skilled, reputable energy healers; or join one of our group healing calls.

If you feel led, you can do the Akashic Records Clearing Meditation that can be found on our meditation app. As mentioned earlier, it will help to clear any blocks, violations, or manipulations that have affected your records.

CHAPTER 45
ACTIVATING AFFIRMATIONS

Many people use affirmations to help in the manifesting process. They reinforce supportive belief system, and help create an energetic link to the goals and experiences you are seeking to create. They can be very powerful tools when spoken with conviction and feeling. All words carry power and vibrational force; so you may want to, use the affirmations to help you stay focused and more in tune with all the words you use, in general. Simply choose to embody the energy and intent of your affirmations throughout the day.

There are many ways to use affirmations; but I have personally found, the most important way to use them, is to create an emotional/spiritual change within yourself. The most powerful affirmations, create an inner click or special feeling when they are spoken. Spend the necessary time to find affirmations that cause an emotional response. Not every affirmation is going to work for everyone. When looking through different affirmations, make sure that they help you believe that you are already experiencing your goals. There are some great websites full of affirmations, and many people are inspired to make up their own. Always use affirmations that specifically address the things you wish to achieve.

Once you have an affirmation, that you have an emotional response to, really do the inner work. Say the affirmation daily, and allow it to go deep within your consciousness to help you.

Feel it. Believe it. Be it.

When doing your affirmations, spend quiet time on a daily basis and breathe deeply. Allow your entire body to relax. Mentally repeat or say your affirmations out loud. Allow the words and meaning to sink down into your being. Harmonize with them.

It's important to really feel and experience the words. Don't just say the words, while parts of you are tuned out or in resistance. If you feel resistance, while saying your affirmations, stay with the emotion; and process through your beliefs. If you continue to feel blocked, find other affirmations to use while working on the blocked/resistant areas. You may even want to receive energetic support from a skilled practitioner to help transmute the blocks.

Don't be afraid to experiment. Make up your own affirmations. What new and different thoughts could help you reach your goals?

Find a way phrase them that will bring you joy and give you a positive emotional feeling. When you say the new phrase, or think the new thought, you will know if its productive for you; because you will be filled with a special joy, even if you don't initially believe, or understand how it will happen. Just be willing to work with it. Remember to always speak your affirmations, in the present tense. Using the present tense, manifests your goals and dreams into the present.

Whatever you are working on, find a sentence that you would be thrilled to say if it were true. Believe that this option for your life already exists, because all aspects of the divine plan exist in the now. Intend to have this or better. Surrender it and then speak the affirmation with conviction.

Use affirmations that you feel a deep connection to. For example:

"I am a child of God. God has my back 100%, and the divine plan for my life is unfailing and unfolding. I am aligning and stepping into it."

"God's light fills every cell in my body. Divine love and light are charging my cells with vibrant health and joy."

"God's bank account is my bank account. I am so grateful that it is overflowing with money, assets, and opportunities. I can spend freely and fearlessly on all I am guided to do."

"God has brought me the most powerful, loving, and joyous relationship. I am deeply touched and constantly inspired to be, so cared for and loved so completely."

"My career is an extension of God's work in the world. I get to have, so much more, fun and joy through staying in divine alignment. I get to uplift others and the planet"

Use some of these. Make up your own. Enjoy the process. As mentioned before, a big part of this is feeling into the emotional body, and making an impact upon the subconscious. It's important and fun, to see what it feels like, to say these things; before you have them. Enjoy holding the intention: you will, one day, have the things you are affirming for; and that you will feel the deepest sense of appreciation and gratitude when you do.

****

Success, supportive friends, abundance, love and vibrant health are my divine birthright. I welcome them and allow them in.

CHAPTER 46
BODY WORK / ENERGY HEALING SESSIONS

When the energy in your body is flowing correctly, it's easier to keep your frequency high, and your mood and thoughts positive. Life is more enjoyable; and sickness (mental, emotional and physical) isn't able to take hold in the same way. Raising your physical body frequency, is a part of raising your overall frequency. Taking time on a daily basis to purposefully and lovingly work with the energy of your physical body, allows you to consistently reach higher vibrations.

There are many different kinds of body work. Receive these gifts to the body as special, pampering, "you time"; that will increase your self-love, self-honoring, and self-care. Your body will thank you, and the quality of your life will increase dramatically.

HOLISTIC EXERCISE / BODY WORK

Holistic exercise and bodywork can be invaluable in helping the body, stay in the highest vibration and the greatest health.

Walking, stretching, swimming, yoga, qigong, tai chi, and similar practices, are all vitalizing to the body. Healing practices such as acupuncture, massage, Feldenkrais and chiropractic adjustments; go a long way in helping to keep the body balanced, free from energetic blockages, and in greater alignment. The more changes you make in your life, the more attentive you want to be with your body; assuring that you are supporting it through the all of the healing processes you are doing.

BREATHWORK

Doing daily breathwork is extremely helpful for maintaining balance, and raising your vibration. Air is the carrier of prana…universal life force energy. And so, when we do breathing exercises, we are intentionally creating a greater connection to Source energy.

There are many different schools of breathwork, and a lot of teachers teaching breathwork online. There are ancient schools of breathwork, such as pranayama from the yogic tradition, and qigong breathing techniques from China. In addition, there are modern teachers embracing newer methods of breathwork. Regardless of what techniques you may feel drawn to, know that seeking to incorporate breathwork into your daily routine can only help. It circulates universal life force energy through your body, oxygenates your blood, relieves stress, re-vibrates your body, and helps you to relax; while increasing your energy, awareness, and focus.

ENERGY HEALING SESSIONS

Receiving energy sessions, from a skilled practitioner, can be one of the most supportive, loving, and helpful things you could ever do for yourself.

The energy sessions that I offer heal: the body, mind, consciousness, etc. They raise the person's frequency, and vibration; remove blockages and attachments; increase the flow of divine energy into the body, and energy field, among other things. This assists in creating and attracting more joy, more success, and vibrant health, etc. Rebalancing and revibrating a person's energy increases their levels of divine alignment, personal power, and personal abundance.

Whatever energy work you do, always consider working directly with the frequency and vibration of your body. As energy beings, the more we understand and influence the way energy flows through our body, the better we can intentionally do for ourselves and others.

CHAPTER 47
VIBRANT, HARMONIZED
LIVING SPACES

Our living spaces and the things we surround ourselves with, make up a huge part our lives. They can uplift us or bring us down, depending on what we have in them and how they're organized. Feng Shui is an ancient Chinese art which harmonizes our living spaces to create optimal environments. It works to create the maximum positive energy flow within our homes and work spaces. This is phenomenal support in creating greater alignment.

The outer reflects the inner. The greater the inner alignment, the more our lives reflect alignment; not only in our environments, but also in our relationships and activities. In the same way that it's important to clear out our subconscious; and hold the vision, energy, and frequency of what we are choosing to create; it's also important to clear out any negative or stagnant energy in our homes and work spaces; so that, we can have the highest vibrations surrounding us.

Without knowing it, we may acquire items and have things in our possession which we no longer want or need, or which are holding negative vibrations. Time goes by. We become busy, and we can sometimes build up clutter. This clutter causes the energy in our lives to stagnate and work against us.

Take a look at the items in your life which may not serve you any longer. Are there things that you no longer need, love, or use that are taking up space in your home? Do you have things that carry other people's energy? Are there things that you enjoyed at one point, but now you don't treasure in the same way?

Consider lovingly releasing any items that are no longer serving you. Perhaps donate them, or give them away. Only introduce items into your home that resonate with who you are now, that you love, and will use. Enjoying all of the items in your home will help you stay in greater alignment; than if the things surrounding you were pulling on your energy, reminding you of other people, and past negative experiences.

We want the things in our home to have the best energy possible. This helps keep the frequencies high. Use sacred woods, sage, or essential oils to keep the energy clear and the fragrances pure and pleasant. Play the prayers of protection if you feel that you have negative energies affecting your space.

Without creating more stress, seek to be as clear and kind as you can when speaking/communicating at home. Keep the verbal negativity to a minimum. No abrasive, harsh, critical language if at all possible. Be mindful of the media and music that you play in your home. The TV shows, music, and movies that you play in your home, all affect the environment. Make sure they make you feel uplifted and good.

Allow your home to be a haven of joy, safety, and serenity. Create routines which allow you to keep your home cleaner without making more work for yourself. Your home is your creation. Allow your home to grow and evolve to match the new reality you are creating. Start by releasing the things that are no longer in alignment with who you are now and who you are becoming.

Some homes have an excess of negative or discordant energy. Depending on the situation, you may need to do house clearings. While I would personally suggest them for everyone, some situations are direr than others. I had a client, with a home that had been built, on land, where many Native Americans had been killed by the colonists. She was experiencing a lot of energy that she couldn't clear, and she didn't know the history of what had happened there. She called me, and asked for help. I was able to see the etheric records, of what had happened, on that land; it left me in tears. I couldn't believe all of the suffering that had been caused, in that one spot, where her house now stood. I worked to escort the souls, of the people that had been killed there, on with their journey into the higher realms. Afterwards, we set up a crystal grid using fine, clear quartz crystals, and a sacred ceremony. In this way, her home was cleared; and the people who had suffered, so needlessly, there were honored and assisted to move on in their spiritual journey.

If you feel like you need help in clearing and resetting the energy of your home, please contact our offices. We sell home clearing kits on our website. It utilizes sacred rituals, angelic assistance, and quartz crystals. The home clearing kit will help to keep your home clear of negative energies and attachments. It will anchor in divine frequencies to maintain the highest possible energy, in your living space, and hold the positive energy in place. This kit can also be used on any building or piece of land. We also have a version, for office spaces, that offers an increased level of support.

Whatever it takes to create the living space, that truly honors who you are, begin doing this today. You will find the joy of living in an environment that has the highest vibrations and energy flow. This is a huge resource in assisting and supporting you, in your life. You will enjoy your home and your time, more. This will substantially increase the quality of your experiences, and your capacity to stay in greater alignment.

CHAPTER 48
ANGELIC TEAMS AND ASSISTANCE

We all have angelic teams and assistance, but we don't always call upon them to help us. The angels are here to help us co-create our lives, and manifest Heaven on Earth. When we call upon them to help us we get exponentially more support, help, and guidance.

I call on them continuously throughout the day. They are actually the backbone of all the healing work that I do. I find their help to be invaluable; they assist with the healings, and they help raise the frequency and vibration, of my clients.

People have different techniques for working with the angels. I respectfully command them.

When you are standing in your full power and authority as a divine being, the divine realm is waiting for your commands and requests. They are here to help you.

Take time to get to know them. If there is one angel that holds special significance, reach out in conversation and prayer. Be willing to have a relationship with the angelic realm. Create a personal bond.

When you call on them, use your senses to feel when they are working with you. Become familiar with what it feels like to have their assistance. They may communicate with you through signs. They may talk to you directly. You may sense their ideas, or see pictures flash in your consciousness. The more you call on them, and work with them directly; the more you will know when they are present, and the more your life will change. They are lovingly awaiting your call. They are here to help you transform your life. This is part of their work. You are not taking their time from more important things.

You can call on them whenever you need, and as much as you feel led. You can call on them for help in your personal life, your career, with your family, or in your personal healing. They can help in all areas.

You may want to start with a daily morning check in with them. Go throughout your day, and talk with them. If you have asked for a particular angel's help, celebrate when you know and can feel your angel's presence.

Humanity and the divine realm were created to work together. When we make the effort they answer.

Get to know them through working with them. You will find, you will create close partnerships and great relationships; that will be lifelong. You will attain alignment, much quicker, through their assistance, and you will have made a bridge into the divine realm; that will help you activate the divine plan in a fun and enjoyable way. I love working with the angels. They have been my constant companions and helpers. It is through their expertise and skill that I am able to stay in alignment, activate the divine plan, and be of the greatest service to the world.

CHAPTER 49
SACRED GEOMETRY

Sacred geometry is known as the architecture of the universe, or the fingerprint of God. It is the universal language of creation, and translates math and numbers into a living force. It provides the key to understanding ancient knowledge, the origins of creation, and our individual DNA. Sacred geometry unlocks the nature of color, sound, light, and love. It is the foundation of divine manifestation into the physical.

Because sacred geometry forms the building blocks of creation; understanding what it is, and how it is in use throughout the cosmos; provides an invaluable resource, in manifesting our goals and dreams. Sacred geometry is found everywhere in nature, and makes up the blueprint of the subatomic world. These structures and forms are what the fabric of life is made out of; when we use them intentionally we step into greater success, and greater alignment in life. Interestingly enough, sacred geometry satisfies: both the left and right brain, both logic and beauty; and flow within it. It is extremely symmetrical, and higher structures can be built out of it; because of the strength and precision of its symmetry.

In the beginning, life began in the form of vibrating sounds, lights and colors. Sacred geometry is the divine motion of spirit creating beauty, harmony, and perfection out of the sacred nothingness. Electromagnetic energy brings in higher frequencies, and solidifies intent into geometric forms; creating the basis of everything in our universe.

The language of sacred geometry exists everywhere in the universe: from human fingerprints, to snowflakes; from pine cones and seashells, to the galaxy; from interlaced tree branches, DNA strands, and chromosomes; to the air, our skin, and our cells. The designs of prehistoric monuments, such as Stonehenge and the pyramids at Giza; as well as the world's greatest religious structures, are based on the principles of sacred geometry. These structures were built by architects; who either worked through the forces of creation, or believed it connected them to the creation source.

Below are some of the sacred geometric forms. Their usefulness will be obvious. Sacred geometry has a correlating aspect in everything that we do.

Years ago musical instruments were all tuned to A=432hz. This is the tuning that was naturally in use, before it was changed in the

1920s to an A=440hz. The 432 tuning is in alignment with the sacred geometry of the planet. Music created with this tuning is known to be more soothing and calming. It allows people to heal, and experience more joy and happiness naturally.

When we moved in to the modern era, the tuning was changed. This change, not coincidentally, corresponds to the expansion of the use of music in many areas in our lives. In the 1920s, we went from the inception of the radio, to the creation of records, to the creation of music videos, to the use of music nearly everywhere we go; ie., in stores, restaurants, offices, gas stations, etc. Changing the tuning in this way causes us to be affected by dissonant tones, which create more agitation and disturbances within us. Surrounded by this form of sound energy, we never really get a chance to fully rebalance and relax.

The sacred geometric forms are all neutral. While they are the building blocks of creation; they can, and have been, used to create negativity by those who understood their power. The forms themselves are nonspecific, and work regardless of the person's intent. Using them to create positive outcomes, carries the added benefit of having divine support.

Sacred Geometry is an extremely important tool. It helps us in regaining our spiritual alignment. It allows us to access higher realms of information. Through it we maintain the atmosphere and frequency of divine creation.

We become aware and aligned with the building blocks of creation, in order to understand how to create as God does.

****

THE SACRED GEOMETRIC FORMS

THE VESICA PISCES

As sound vibration unfolds in various forms, it begins with an orb around a central point; otherwise known as, the void or absence of matter.

The circle reflects awareness and knowledge through duplicating itself. This reflection of the circle's own image creates the Vesica Pisces.

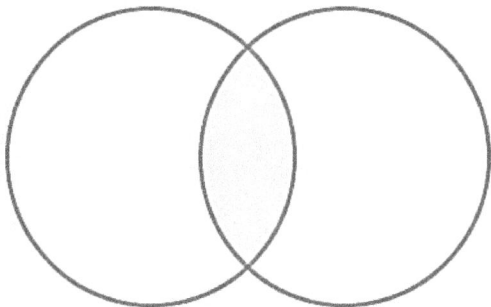

As a circle replicates into its exact likeness, the two circles intersect to create a fish, or pisces, in their center.

THE SEED OF LIFE

The Seed of Life represents the cycles of life and reflects fertility, reproduction, and creativity. It signifies new beginnings. The cycle of creation continues as the seed replicates.

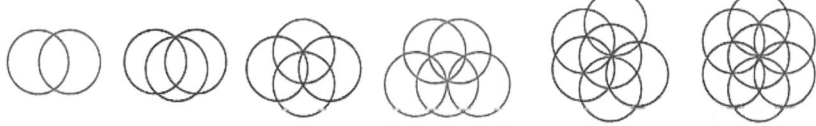

The seven circles within the seed of life create circles and shapes which replicate to intersect and form the flower of life, the creation pattern of all things in existence.

THE FLOWER OF LIFE

The Flower of Life is represented in every culture on the planet, and is known as the physical manifestation of spirit. It expands in a process that occurs in every organism on earth; and as it splits, it replicates itself in the manner of cell reproduction.

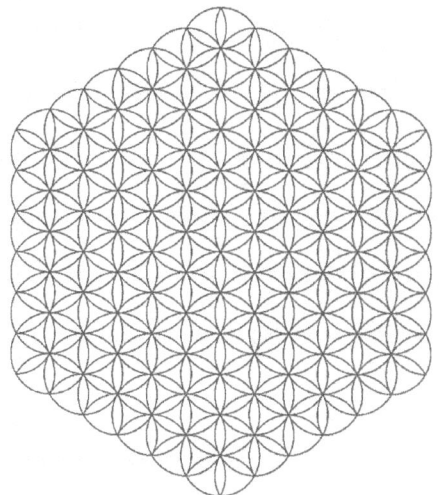

The Flower of Life represents sacred feminine energy, or yang, for its ability to replicate. Like the spiral orb and circle, it represents the creative, intuitive, right brain aspect of life.

From the Flower of Life a structure emerges known as Metatron's cube, a three dimensional grid that forms the structure of our cosmos.

METATRON'S CUBE

Metatron's Cube is the matrix which forms the structure of 3-dimensional reality, the analytical, left brain qualities of life; or the masculine yin as it relates to the square, angled structures.

Yet the flower of life and Metatron's cube are united, and can only create and expand as one. Together they represent the unity of male and female aspects, or the universal divine. One cannot exist without the other. Together they represent expanding consciousness and the potency of life.

THE FIVE PLATONIC SOLIDS

A platonic solid is a third dimensional shape with equal sides meeting at their corners. There are only five of these forms: the tetrahedron, the cube, the octahedron, the dodecahedron, and the icosahedron.

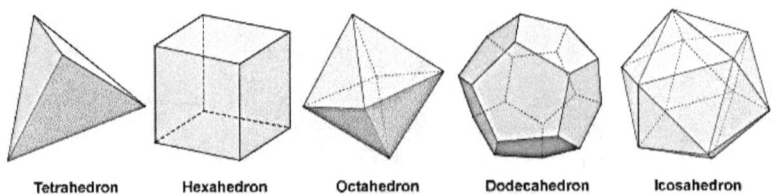

Tetrahedron   Hexahedron   Octahedron   Dodecahedron   Icosahedron

All five platonic solids, are found within metatron's cube and the flower of life, which, together, form the building blocks of life.

FIBONACCI SEQUENCE

Out of the infinitely expanding pattern of Metatron's Cube and the Flower of Life, comes the Fibonacci sequence; a relation of numbers intimately connected to and central to the creation process. As one cell divides into two, two then become four, eight then become sixteen, and so on; the sequence is:

1, 1, 2, 3, 5, 8, 13, 21, 34, 55, 89, 144, 233, etc……. to infinitum.

Each number is the sum of the numbers before it.

1+1=2
1+2=3
2+3=5
3+5=8

And so on, without measurable end.

1+1=2
1+2=3
2+3=5
3+5=8
5+8=13
8+13=21

13+21=34
21+34=55
34+55=89
55+89=144
89+144=233
144+233=377
etc.,

THE FIBONACCI SPIRAL

Two successive Fibonacci Numbers form a ratio when measured against another. To get the ratio, divide the second number by the first.

3/2=1.5

5/3=1.666....

8/5=1.6

When charted on a graph, the ratios create a spiral.

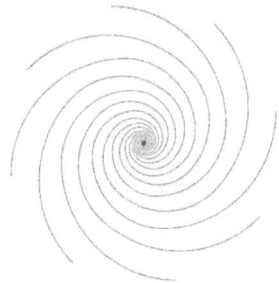

The Fibonacci Spiral shows up in all forms of life: flowers, seeds, pine cones, shells, weather formations, ocean waves, faces, honey bees, and the human body, to name a few.

The Giza Pyramids are placed in the form of the Fibonacci Spiral.

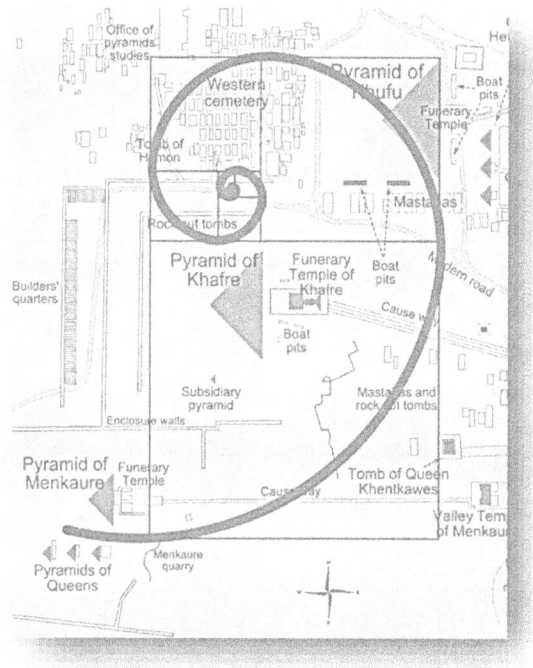

THE GOLDEN RATIO

The Fibonacci Sequence leads to the Golden Ratio of 1.61803, which is a divine proportion commonly found in nature - the ratio of 1 to 1.618. It's also referred to as the divine proportion, Fibonacci number, or phi.

The golden ratio is often depicted by a sequence of rectangles and squares that replicate indefinitely, and fit perfectly within one another.

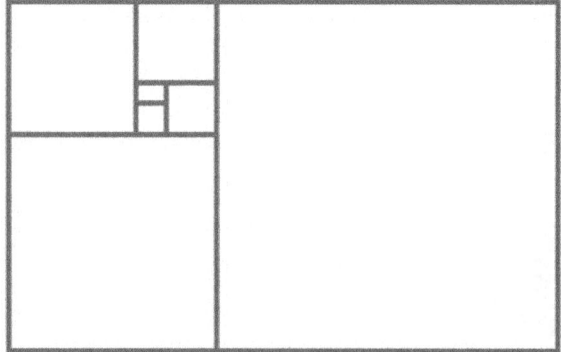

The digits of the Golden Ratio go on into infinity:

1.618033988749894848420....

MERKABA (Mer-Ka-Ba) or STAR TETRAHEDRON

The Merkaba consists of two equal tetrahedrons, or three sided pyramids; one facing up, one facing down, locked together, in constant rotation. As they spin in different directions, they form a matrix of high vibrational light energy. Once found atop every pyramid, the Merkabas were removed by those trying to prevent humanity's ascendance. They are the true ark of the covenant. The bible says, when you gaze upon the ark of the covenant, you get burned. This is because the Merkaba on top of every pyramid was made of crystal, and operated like a lens, which burned the corneas of those who gazed at it. To stop this, they covered the Merkabas with a film of gold leaf, that was the same vibration as the crystal. Gold vibrates at the same frequency as water and crystal.

There are three Merkaba fields around each human being, with the center point of the Merkaba field located at the sacrum where life began. When you spin your Merkaba fields in three counter rotations, your energy and vibration accelerates. When used during meditation, the Merkaba transports your consciousness to higher dimensions.

Spelled Merkavah in the Torah, it is referenced as a "chariot", and the "Throne of God", further clarifying that the Merkabah is the vehicle of ascendance. It was used by Ezekiel to ascend to the God Realm.

The Merkaba is a symbol used for protection and divine light. Technically, it is an electromagnetic field that extends through all dimensions; surrounding the human body, protecting it, and raising its vibration. It both transmits and receives energy.

CHAPTER 50
THE DIVINE LAWS

So much of the current manifesting movement is driven by the law of attraction. This is only one law; however, in the midst of the other divine laws that are continuously in operation. So many people are only focused on this law, as opposed to all of them; many times, their manifesting process is unbalanced. They don't fully reap the benefits of what they are seeking to create. They put in a lot of time and energy; they may end up frustrated, if it doesn't happen in a timely fashion or it doesn't happen at all. At the same time, they act without the awareness of the other laws, which can substantially increase their success and alignment. It's like having a chair with only one leg. It's difficult to gain balance. It's difficult to sit on it. It's difficult to use.

Inversely, consciously using all of the laws, as opposed to using only one, will help to create greater success and movement in life.

There are many sites online which talk more extensively about the divine laws. Do your research. Find out about these other laws. Understanding how they all work together will help you integrate the intricacies of the manifesting process and gain greater mastery.

Ultimately, divine law is founded upon unconditional love. The ability to move through all you do, say, and feel; immersed in unconditional love, is the highest way of staying in alignment with divine law.

In the midst of, and surrounding all of these laws is Divine Grace. Grace can happen under any circumstance. Some would say, Grace is happening all of the time; regardless, of how we are perceiving events. Grace is something to stay in gratitude over and to have the deepest sense of reverence for. Grace is the hand of God functioning in the midst of the different situations you're experiencing. It's important to notice how the Divine is working in your life, and how Grace is flowing in the midst of all you are seeking to achieve.

Some of the divine laws are:

THE LAW OF CAUSE AND EFFECT

What you release into the world comes back to you; at least the essence of the experience is returned to you. Every action brings an equal reaction; always, with the same kind of energy that was initially offered. If you are sending out positive energy, the essence of this energy and experience will return to you. If you are sending out mean-spirited or negative energy, the essence of this will be returned to you. Each person is completely responsible for what is brought back to them through the words, thoughts, and deeds they send out. You are the one who is orchestrating what kind of energy is in your experience, beauty, or lightness; heaviness or anger. Many times people call this karma. And, indeed karma is a sanskrit word, which means action. The result of your actions is what returns to you.

THE LAW OF MENTAL EQUIVALENTS

What you think about and visualize, manifests into your reality. Thoughts are made from energy, and they manifest themselves into the physical. You go as far as your thoughts can take you.

THE LAW OF PERSONAL CHOICE

Everyone has the freedom to choose; what they do, say, and experience. God will not violate this. If you want help from God; you have to ask for it, and you have to choose to accept help.

THE LAW OF CORRESPONDENCE

As above, so below. Inner to outer. This law states that the inner reflects the outer, and the outer reflects the inner. The spiritual is reflected in the material, and the material is reflected in the spiritual.

THE LAW OF PERSONAL RESPONSIBILITY

Your life is your responsibility. If you create something, you must take responsibility for it. If you want things to change, you must step forward and make these changes. Create positive situations, and work with the best people so that you can move forward in your life. Take responsibility for what is going on in your life, and if you need to make changes, make them.

THE LAW OF ATTRACTION

We are magnetic beings; we attract things, situations, and people in to our life based on our predominant belief, frequency, and thoughts. Consciously align your frequency, belief, emotions, and intention with what you are seeking to create; and it will come to you in greater ease and grace.

THE LAW OF ENERGY

The law of energy states: manifestation happens according to the nature of the energy, frequency and vibration held. Negative frequencies manifest at a slower rate, and manifest negative experiences. Positive energies manifest at a faster rate; in turn, manifest positive things.

There is a whole spectrum of experiences that fall in between the positive and the negative; which, in turn, yields various results.

THE LAW OF ACHIEVEMENT

The law of achievement says: everyone was born to achieve success. Each person has, within them, the blueprint to succeed in their life. We literally carry, within us, the programing to succeed. It has been guaranteed because of this blueprint. It is divine will. It is up to us to align ourselves with this understanding: so the Divine can move through us, and create our highest, most satisfying, life.

THE LAW OF ALIGNMENT

The law of alignment says: the more we are in alignment with divine law, the more the universe will be in alignment with us. We can achieve divine alignment faster, through honoring the spiritual laws in our daily lives.

THE LAW OF ABUNDANCE

The entire cosmos is a source of endless abundance. There is more than enough for everyone. All we have to do, is tune into the abundance that is already in existence, and an increase of abundance will flow into our lives faster. There is no limit to the goodness we can experience. Open yourself to receive it all.

CHAPTER 51
MAGI MANIFESTING TECHNIQUE

In the ancient stories, after the fall of humanity…a being by the name of Melchizedek came to the Earth from the Melchizedek Realm, the Ultimate Dimension, to help people reclaim their divinity and live the life the Creator intended for them. He came to help people achieve Christ Consciousness, live in divine alignment, access the divine plan of their lives, and have a committed relationship with God. Melchizedek came to help the planet move into the fifth dimension.

He started a series of mystery schools that began in Egypt and spread all over the Middle East into Persia. These mystery schools taught people how to use the energy of unconditional of love to restore their own power and live as divine beings. The priests who were educated, through these mystery schools, were considered to be the most advanced teachers of the time. They dedicated themselves to establishing divine order, within their own lives, so they could directly assist humanity in doing the same.

A key precept for the Magi priests is a working knowledge of all of the divine laws. The three kings in the Christ Story were Magi priests. Jesus was the high priest of the Magi order. After his birth, the Magi priests were led to him by a star in the sky.

The following is a Magi manifesting technique based on seeding your intention into sacred geometry. It breaks through all AI, radionics, and negativity which are interfering with people's creativity. It allows them to harness more divine energy and use it to manifest their dreams while receiving divine assistance.

This particular technique uses angelic writing and a five pointed star known as a pentagram which has 5 pyramids on it that make up the star points. Remember that sacred geometry is powerful, yet neutral. There are those who are positive who use it. There are those who are negative who use it. But the structure itself, is neither good nor bad. It is a tool to assist in the creative process. You must attach your intention to it. In this way, it works to accelerate the manifestation of your goals.

It's important to explain how pyramids work before discussing the technique. Pyramids are natural energy accelerators. Those who built the pyramids understood the power of sacred geometry to harness and amplify. Pyramids raise the frequency and vibration of anyone inside of them. They also raise the frequency of the planet.

(1) The energy flows down around the base of the pyramid and starts to zig zag across the interior of the base.

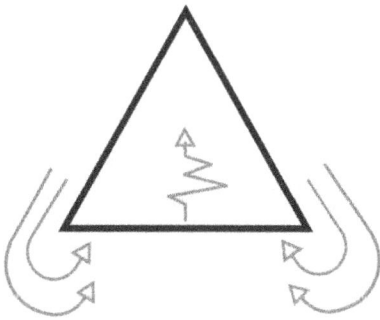

(2) The energy rises in a zig zag picking up speed and rising in frequency.

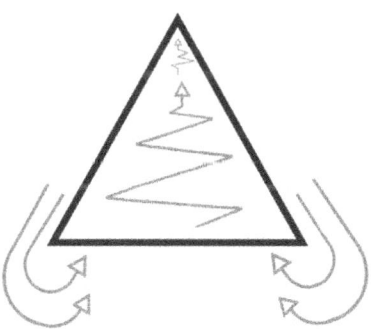

(3) The energy expands at the top and fires down through the center.

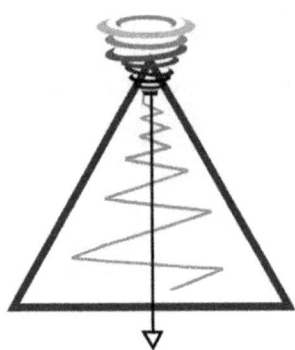

In ancient Egypt, the king's chamber was always directly underneath this line of downward energy. Meditating in the king's chamber is extremely helpful; whoever is in the chamber receives highly accelerated energy.

MAGI MANIFESTING TECHNIQUE

What you will need:
- A single piece of paper for each goal you are seeking to manifest
- A pen
- A burning bowl
- 45 minutes to an hour for the whole process from start to finish for each goal

It's important to have your dream/goal broken down into what I call the 5 "W"s. Who? What? Where? When? Why?
It's important to state:

who is making the request or working on the goal,
what the goal is,
where the manifestation needs to take place,
when it needs to take place and
why it is an important goal.

After you get clear about this, take out your pen and paper.

(1) With a single stroke, not lifting the pen off of the paper, create a five pointed star.

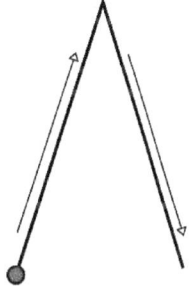 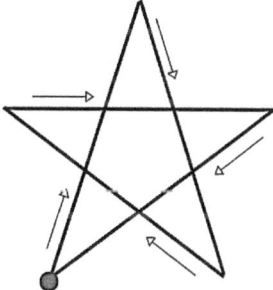

(2) Start at a point close to the top, and label the points, and proceed clockwise. Who? What? Where? When? Why?

(3) Next to each word write out the corresponding information. Suppose your name is Sarah and you want a new car, (specifically list the kind, make and model), to transport your family around in. You would write out next to the 5 "W"s the following information:

Who? Sarah
What? A new car (list the kind-make and model)
Where? In my driveway
When? In the now
Why? To transport my family around
So again…

- Who? Next to this write the name of the person seeking to manifest. If it is you, write your name out next to it.
- What? Write out what you want.
- Where? Write out where you want the manifestation to occur. If you want money, write out that you want it in your bank account.
- When. Always write…"In The Now"'
- Why? Next to this one write the purpose for having it and how it will serve you, your loved ones, and humanity. You can say, "For my upliftment, and for the upliftment of the planet".

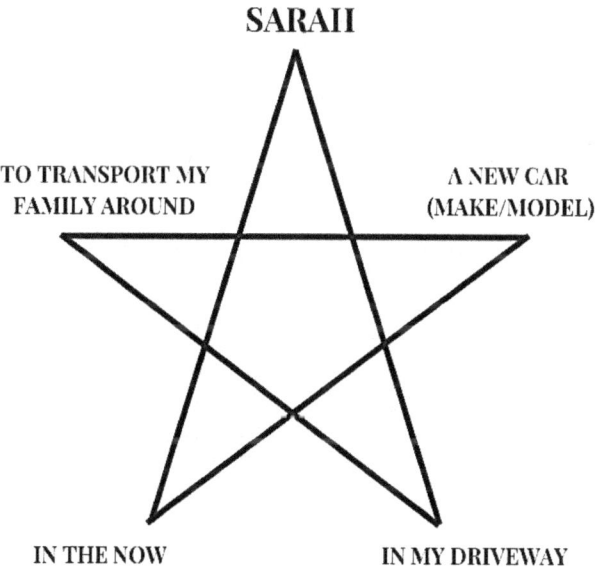

(4) Then go back and write each word backwards underneath the original word. For example, in the " WHEN" section, "In The Now"...written backwards will read: "won eht ni".

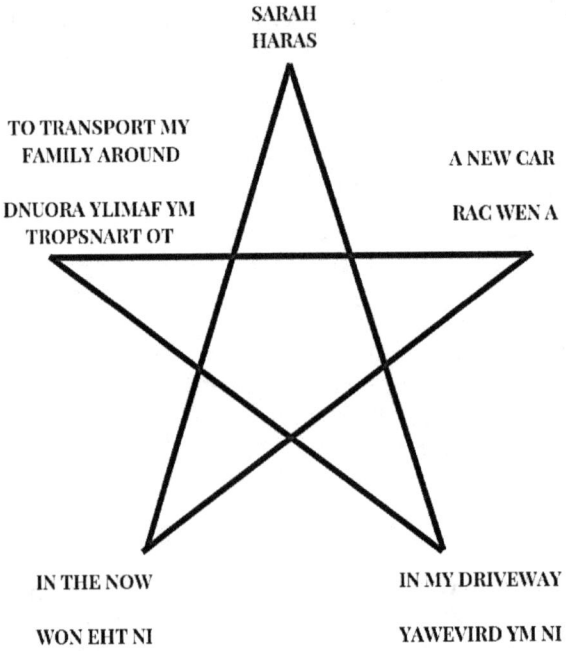

(5) The next step is to take the angelic writing chart and under the backwards writing, write the corresponding angelic letter under each letter. You can find an attached copy of angelic writing at the end of this chapter.

(6) It's important to understand these last steps...specifically, how and why this process works. When you seed your intent onto the star points...you are actually seeding your intent onto 5 pyramids. On paper they are 2 dimensional and are triangles. Seeding this energy on to each point creates an exponentially powerful process that brings all of the energy from the 5 pyramids together; when they fire the energy down from the top they meet in the middle, and accelerate even more before they fire out into the divine realm.

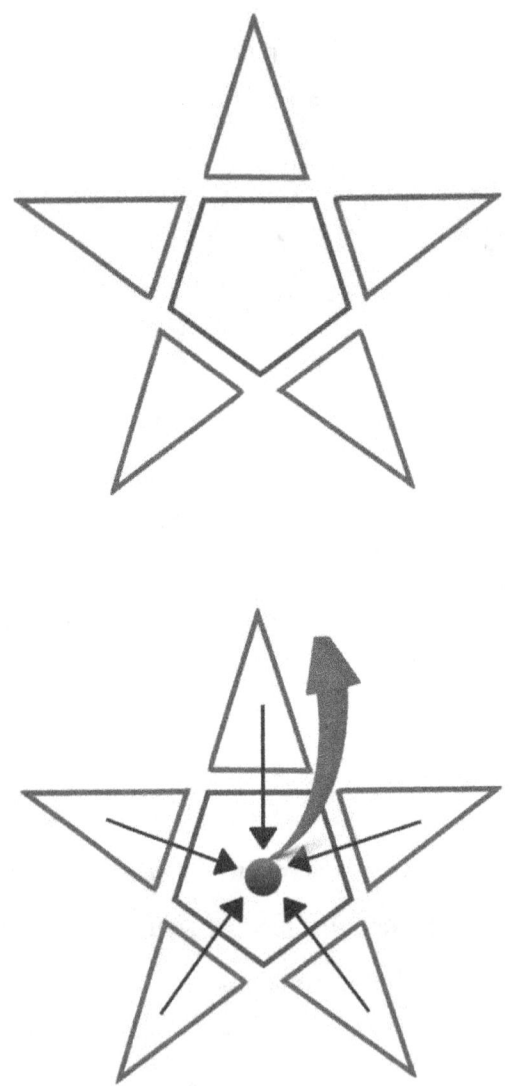

Once you have all of the writing, in the three different ways, written out around the pentagon; hold the paper in your hand and say the following prayer with calm, certain, authority.

PRAYER TO RELEASE THE MANIFESTATION TO THE UNIVERSE

I am of God. I ground myself to the Earth.
In the Name of All That is Holy,
Dear God, I release this manifestation to You and the Universe.
This is my manifestation:
(Read the 5 "W"s from the paper.)

I release it to You now.

(Burn the paper in a safe container like a burning bowl.)

I thank You God and The Universe and I send You my Unconditional Love.
So Be It / Amen.

Once you burn the paper, follow all of the synchronicities and prompts brought to you by the universe. Take action in any way you are guided. Your manifestation will come to you in the right way, at the right time, in perfect order.

www.ingramcontent.com/pod-product-compliance
Lightning Source LLC
Chambersburg PA
CBHW052041220426
43663CB00012B/2403